Red Jacket

THE
Iroquois
AND THEIR
NEIGHBORS

Laurence M. Hauptman, *Series Editor*

Portrait of Red Jacket by John Lee Mathies, 1820.
*Courtesy of the Memorial Art Gallery of the
University of Rochester and the estate of John W. Brown.*

Red Jacket

IROQUOIS DIPLOMAT AND ORATOR

Christopher Densmore

SYRACUSE UNIVERSITY PRESS

First Edition 1999

99   00   01   02   03   04   6   5   4   3   2   1

This book is published with the assistance
of the John Ben Snow Foundation.

The paper used in this publication meets the minimum requirements of
American National Standard for Information Sciences—Permanence of
Paper for Printed Library Materials, ANSI Z39.48-1984. ∞™

Library of Congress Cataloging-in-Publication Data
Densmore, Christopher.
Red Jacket : Iroquois diplomat and orator / Christopher Densmore.
p.   cm — (The Iroquois and their neighbors)
Includes bibliographical references and index.
ISBN 0-8156-2785-8 (cloth : alk. paper).—ISBN 0-8156-0548-X
(pbk. : alk. paper)
1. Red Jacket (Seneca chief), ca. 1756–1830.   2. Seneca Indians—
Kings and rulers—Bibliography.   3. Seneca Indians—Politics and
government.   4. Seneca Indians—Government relations.   I. Title.
II. Series.
E99.S3R289   1998
973'.049755—dc21
[B]   98-29828

Manufactured in the United States of America

To my family for their love and support:
Laura, Bronwen, Ezekiel, *and* Ruth Densmore

Christopher Densmore is Director of the University Archives, University at Buffalo. He is coeditor of *Quaker Crosscurrents: Three Hundred Years of Friends in the New York Yearly Meetings* and author of a number of articles on the Society of Friends (Quakers) in New York State and Canada, on relations between Quakers and Native Americans in New York State, and on archival administration. He is a former chair of the Lake Ontario Archives Conference and currently chair of the Canadian Friends Historical Association.

Contents

Illustrations

Acknowledgments

I wish to acknowledge the advice of several scholars of Iroquois culture, including Laurence M. Hauptman, Carl F. Benn, and Wallace F. Chafee; the assistance of colleagues in Libraries and Special Collections, particularly the Interlibrary Loan Department at Lockwood Library, University at Buffalo, and Patricia Virgil and Mary Bell at the Buffalo and Erie County Historical Society; to Daniel Hennessey for drafting the maps; and finally the editorial advice and assistance of Karen Kuehmeier, Corrine Koepf, and Daniel DiLandro.

Introduction

The speech delivered by Red Jacket (1758-1830) to Jacob Cram, a Christian missionary at Buffalo Creek in western New York in 1805, is perhaps the most often reprinted composition by a Native American author. In this speech Red Jacket contrasts the treatment of the whites by the Indians with the treatment of his own people. When whites first came to the New World seeking refuge from persecution, the Indians took pity on them and gave them corn, meat, and a place to stay. In return, the whites gave the Indians poison (liquor) and took away their lands. Not being content with land, Red Jacket told the missionary, the whites now wanted to force their religion on the Indians. The Indians, Red Jacket asserted, had their own religion, given to them by the Great Spirit, who knew what was best for his children. Nevertheless, Red Jacket proposed an experiment. He suggested that Cram try Christianity on the Senecas' white neighbors. "If we find it does them good, makes them honest and less disposed to cheat Indians; we will then consider of what you have said."

Red Jacket was a member of the Seneca Nation, the westernmost nation of the powerful Six Nations of the Iroquois Confederacy. For almost one century before Red Jacket's birth the Iroquois had been a major power in North

America during the struggles between France and Britain during the seventeenth and eighteenth centuries, and their support was anxiously solicited by both sides. During the American Revolution the rebellious colonists and the British government courted the Iroquois. After the Revolution the political fortunes of the Iroquois Confederacy rapidly declined. It was Red Jacket's fate to fight the diplomatic battle for the Senecas to retain their lands, their sovereignty, and their culture as the white settlers poured into the old Iroquois lands in New York.

The Iroquois have a strong tradition of oratory, and Red Jacket was an orator. He participated in the political affairs of the Senecas and the Iroquois from the beginning of the American Revolution in 1775 until his death in 1830, fifty-five years later. Between the 1790s and the 1820s Red Jacket frequently spoke on behalf of the Six Nations—or more precisely, the portion of the Six Nations remaining in New York after the American Revolution. He spoke in negotiations with the United States, with the government of British North America, with New York State, and between the Iroquois in New York State and their fellow Iroquois in Canada. During that time Red Jacket met with most, if not all, of the American presidents from George Washington to Andrew Jackson. With the publication and frequent reprintings of his speeches against missionaries and land agents, particularly after 1810, Red Jacket became a figure in American folk culture.

Red Jacket's importance comes from his skill as an orator. During his lifetime white men sometimes portrayed Red Jacket as a hereditary chieftain and a great warrior. He was neither. In fact, his own people teased him about his distinct disinclination to fight during the American Revolution. His authority derived from his political skills, and more importantly, from his ability to express the sentiments of his people in council. These skills drew on the traditions of the Iroquois.

When Red Jacket spoke in council, he was expressing the feelings of his constituents. The words were Red Jacket's, but the sentiments were those of the larger body. His expressions and imagery drew from the rich culture of Iroquois diplomacy. It is not until after 1817, when the Senecas divided into the so-called Christian and Pagan Parties that one can clearly distinguish the personal opinions of Red Jacket from those of his nation.

Red Jacket often spoke for the Six Nations or the Seneca Nation in negotiations with the whites. In the popular mind he was widely regarded as the leader of the Seneca Nation, and Red Jacket, an ambitious man, seemed to have used every opportunity to enlarge his reputation. In fact, his political power among his own people was limited. Among the Senecas who lived in the Buffalo Creek Reservation (near the modern city of Buffalo, New York), Red Jacket appears to have been less influential in local political affairs than Farmer's Brother, Young King, or Captain Pollard. His power and authority in negotiations with whites and other Indians rested on his skill as an orator and diplomat, not on his political rank within his own tribe and community.

In this biography I refer to him as Red Jacket, his name among the whites. His Seneca name has usually been given as Sagoyewatha, meaning "Keeper Awake" or "He Who Keeps Them Awake." The decision to use his English name is deliberate. Nearly all of the available documentation on his career comes from English language sources. Red Jacket knew little English and as a matter of policy never used even that little in negotiations or in public statements. Historians do not, in fact, have Red Jacket's actual speeches; they have versions of those speeches as translated and recorded by white people. They know much about Red Jacket, the man who met with the whites in council, but they know relatively little about Sagoyewatha, the Seneca.

I frequently use the term *white men* rather than *Euroamerican* and *Indian* rather than *Native American*. Neither term is precise, but they were the terms used at the time and it seems anachronistic to have Red Jacket denouncing the failings of "Euroamericans." In later chapters I use *Pagan* to refer to a faction of the Senecas supported—and to a large extent headed—by Red Jacket during the 1820s. The usage is based on the contemporaneous language (in the white man's accounts). Not all members of the Christian Party were necessarily Christians, nor were all adherents of the Pagan Party necessarily traditionalists in matters of religion. The absence of women in my account of Red Jacket is also a problem. Although white women had almost no voice in the political affairs and diplomacy of the young United States, Iroquois women not only held considerable political power but selected and could depose the (male) chiefs and sachems and participated in councils, particularly when the issues involved land and the general welfare of the people. On several occasions Red Jacket acted as speaker for the women. The absence of women from this story reflects the absence of women from the documentation as recorded by non-Indian (male) observers. It does not reflect Iroquois reality.

There is considerable documentation about Red Jacket. He was a famous man, particularly after the publication of some of his speeches. Whites were anxious to meet him and to record anecdotes of his career. Sketches of Red Jacket and selections from his speeches were featured in the popular collections of Indian biographies by Thomas Drake and William Thatcher (both first published in 1832). Red Jacket was the first of the famous chiefs depicted in Thomas L. McKenney and James Hall's *History of the Indian Tribes of North America* (1838).

William Leete Stone (1792–1844), a journalist and historian, intended to write a history of the Six Nations. His biography of the Mohawk leader Joseph Brant was published in 1838, followed by *The Life and Times of Red Jacket* in 1841. A second edition of Stone's book, retitled *The Life and Times of Sa-go-ye-wat-ha, or Red Jacket* was issued in 1866 but contains only minor changes. Stone's book has remained the major source on the life of Red Jacket. J. Niles Hubbard's *An Account of Red Jacket and His People* (1886) largely follows Stone but does include some details gathered by Hubbard from Seneca and non-Seneca informants. Arthur C. Parker's *Red Jacket: Last of the Seneca* (1952) was written as a popular biography without footnotes but draws on Parker's long research into the history of the Six Nations.

Contemporaneous Native American accounts of Red Jacket are rare. Governor Blacksnake (1753?–1859), Red Jacket's cousin and contemporary, was interviewed twice late in his life and provided brief but very important details about Red Jacket's family background and activities during the American Revolution. Nathaniel T. Strong (ca. 1810–1872), a Seneca chief, delivered a speech on Red Jacket in 1863 that contained information on Red Jacket's early life found nowhere else. The manuscript of this speech is preserved in the Buffalo and Erie County Historical Society. Important contemporary accounts by white men are found in the papers and recollections of Thomas Morris, preserved in the Henry O'Reilly Collection, Papers Relating to the Six Nations, at the New-York Historical Society; in the Timothy Pickering Papers at the Massachusetts Historical Society; and in the United States National Archives.

Despite the great interest in Red Jacket, particularly during the last decade of his life, it is difficult to pin down important details of his life. At least five locations have been named as his birthplace, and his birth date has variously been given as 1750, 1751–52, 1756, and 1758. In some accounts he is described as a league chief or sachem, whereas equally authoritative accounts say that he never held that position. Even the facts surrounding his death and burial in 1830 are disputed. The documentation is uneven, and the accounts of major events often rest largely and sometimes exclusively on a single source. Most of what is known about the negotiations at the Treaty of Big Tree in 1797 derive from accounts by Thomas Morris, Red Jacket's opponent in those negotiations. The account of the "trial" of Red Jacket, circa 1802, is based on an account by New York Governor DeWitt Clinton written several years later. Clinton was not present at that event. In many cases, it is now impossible to state even basic facts with certainty although I have strived to present what in my judgment is plausible and consistent with the known facts.

This biography is not the final word on Red Jacket, much less the final word on Sagoyewatha. History is not a collection of facts but an interpretation of them. Red Jacket was a complex person with a good amount of vanity and self-interest in his makeup. It would be possible to draw a picture of a more heroic Red Jacket, and it would be equally possible to debunk the mythology of Red Jacket by focusing on his contradictions and inconsistencies, particularly in the earlier years of his career. While not ignoring his failings—or, perhaps more accurately, the stories of those failings spread by his opponents—I believe that a full examination of Red Jacket's life reinforces the picture of Red Jacket as the defender of Seneca traditions and lands against the attacks of land speculators and missionaries.

Red Jacket's principal objectives were to preserve the Seneca title to their lands in New York, to assert Seneca sovereignty over their internal affairs, and to defend Seneca customs and traditions against those who believed that the Indians needed to adopt fully the white man's ways and the white man's religion. There were times during Red Jacket's lifetime, and again in the late 1830s and early 1840s, when it looked as if the Senecas would have to leave New York or would lose their cultural identity under pressure to assimilate with white culture. In evaluating Red Jacket's legacy it is critical to remember that today Senecas live on the Cattaraugus, Alleghany, and Tonawanda reservations within New York State on lands that were theirs before the arrival of the whites, with rights stemming from a treaty negotiated by Red Jacket and others more than two centuries ago, under Seneca governments, and with a strong sense of cultural identity and continuity. Red Jacket's goal was survival, and the Senecas have survived.

Indian Names

The following is a list of forms of Indian personal and place names used in the text. The original source documents used for this book contain many variant spellings of these names. I have employed the most authoritative sources available to me, or in some cases used the most common form of a name. The list contains only Indian names in Indian languages, and does not include the names recognizable in English (like Jemison, Jones, or Parker).

Abeel	Cornplanter (also O'Baill)
Allegany	Reservation
Allegheny	River
Ahweyneyohn	Red Jacket's mother
Canadaseagoe	Variant of Kanatasake
Canawaugus	Village near Avon
Canadaway	Creek, northeast Chautauqua
Caneadea	Reservation on Genesee River
Canoga	Red Jacket's birthplace
Chippawa	Battle, location in Canada
Chippewa	Tribe
Conewagus	Variant of Canawaugus
Degeney	Red Jacket's wife

Deseronto	Mohawk reservation in Canada
Ganodesaga	Variant of Kanataske
Ga-no-geh	Variant of Canoga
Gardeau	Reservation on Genesee [Wallace]
Go yo so doh	Red Jacket's subsachem name
Ha-wen-iu	The "Master Spirit"
Haudenosaunee	The League (variant)
Ho-dé-no-sau-nee	The League (variant)
Hodenosaunee	The League (variant)
Houdenosaunee	The League (variant)
Kanadesaga	Variant of Kanataske
Kanataske	Village near Geneva
Kau-qua-tau	Seneca woman, executed as a witch
Messaquakenoe	Painted Pole
Ne-do-cio-weh-ah	Little Vale of Basswoods
Oh-no-syo-dyno	Abby Jacket
Otetiani	Red Jacket's childhood name
Oyongwongyeh	Creek, east of Fort Niagara [variant]
Oyonwayea	Creek, east of Fort Niagara [variant]
Quatoghies	Wyandot Indians
Saco-que-y-wan-tau	Variant of Red Jacket
Sagoyewatha	Preferred spelling of Red Jacket
Sa-go-ye-wat-ha	Variant of Red Jacket
Sagu-yu-what-ha	Variant of Red Jacket
Sa-gu-yu-what-ha	Variant of Red Jacket
Shagóye:wa:tha?	Wallace Chafee's spelling of Red Jacket
Sho-gyo-a-ja-ach	John Jacket
Skoiyase	Village near Waterloo, N.Y.
So-son-do-wa	Edward Cornplanter

Sosehawa	Jemmy Johnson
Soonongize	Tommy-Jemmy
Tecumseh	Western Indian leader
Tehoseroron	Buffalo Creek
Tenskawantowa	Shawnee Prophet, Tecumseh's brother
Thadahwahnyeh	Red Jacket's father
Tyendinaga	Variant of Deserto
Waahagadek	Red Jacket's Wife
Wyashoh	Red Jacket's first wife, according to Arthur Parker
Yahahweeh	Red Jacket's daughter-in-law (no English version)
Yau-go-ya-yat-haw	Variant of Red Jacket

Abbreviations

ASPIA	*American State Papers. Indian Affairs.*
Amer. Speaker	*American Speaker*
BHS	Buffalo Historical Society
LLHS	Lundy's Lane Historical Society
NYYM	New York Yearly Meeting
PYM	Philadelphia Yearly Meeting
Reg. of Debates	*Register of Debates in Congress*
US/SW/IA/LS	United States. Records of the Office of the Secretary of War Relating to Indian Affairs. Letters Sent.
US/SW/IA/LR	United States. Records of the Office of the Secretary of War Relating to Indian Affairs. Letters Received.

US/WD/IA/LR (Seneca) — United States. War Department. Office of Indian Affairs. Letters Received. Seneca Agency in New York.

US/WD/IA/LR (Six Nations) — United States. War Department. Office of Indian Affairs. Letters Received. Six Nations Agency.

US/WD/IA/LS — United States. War Department. Office of Indian Affairs. Letters Sent.

Red Jacket

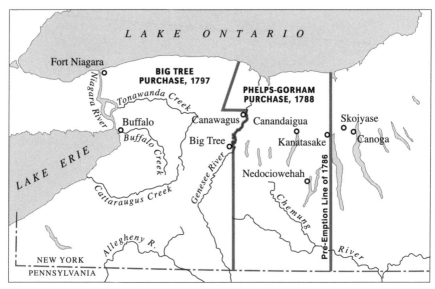

Seneca–Cayuga Territory, ca. 1760–1797

1

———

Before the Whirlwind,
1758–1775

Red Jacket was born in the 1750s, probably 1758, in the Finger Lakes Region of what is today New York State. He was a member of the Seneca Nation, and the Senecas were the "keepers of the western door" for the powerful Iroquois Confederacy. The Confederacy consisted of the Six Nations: Mohawk, Oneida, Onondaga, Cayuga, Tuscarora, and Seneca. White settlement ended at German Flats, now Herkimer, eighty miles west of Albany. The rest of what is today New York State, west and north, was the land of the Six Nations, and the authority of the Six Nations extended south into Pennsylvania and west into the vast Ohio country.

The Iroquois name for themselves was transcribed by Lewis Henry Morgan (1851) as Ho-de'-no-sau-nee. The contemporary spelling varies: Houdenosaunee (Jennings 1985, xiii), Haudenosaunee (Venables 1995, viii), Hodenosaunee (Snow 1994, 60). The name means "People of the Longhouse" because the confederacy was like the traditional longhouse dwelling of the Iroquois. In the longhouse several families lived in a common structure, within which each family had its own place. In the metaphorical longhouse of the confederacy, the Mohawks, who lived closest to the whites (and in the Mohawk valley were interspersed with white settlements)

were the "keepers of the eastern door." The Seneca were the
farthest west and, hence, were the "keepers of the western
door." In between the Seneca were the Oneidas, Onondagas,
Cayugas, and Tuscaroras. The boundary between the Seneca
Nation and the Cayugas ran north to south between Seneca
Lake and Cayuga Lake. Seneca villages were located across
western New York and in northern Pennsylvania, with the
major settlements at the northern ends of Seneca and
Canandaigua Lakes, and along the Genesee River Valley.

By the 1820s Red Jacket was a famous man, and visitors
to western New York sought him out. People who knew
Red Jacket, even those who knew people who knew Red
Jacket, were interviewed by local historians in the 1830s and
after. This resulted in a sizable body of information about
Red Jacket although much of it is contradictory and some
of it very dubious.

Several places in New York have been identified as Red
Jacket's birthplace. Thomas L. McKenney, who, as head of
the Bureau of Indian Affairs in the 1820s had occasion to
learn about and meet with Red Jacket, wrote that Red
Jacket had been born at Old Castle near Geneva, New York
(McKenney, 1967, 3). McKenney's statement was accepted by
the later biographers of Red Jacket, William L. Stone (1841,
18) and J. Niles Hubbard (1886, 10). Red Jacket's cousin and
contemporary, Governor Blacksnake (1753?–1859), told historian Lyman Draper in 1850 that Red Jacket was born at
Canadaseagoe or "New Town" (Draper Manuscripts, S-4-
74). Nathaniel T. Strong (1810?–1872), the Seneca son of
Captain Strong, said that Red Jacket's birthplace was the
village called Ganodesaga (Strong, 1863, 3). Both Canadaseagoe and Ganodesaga appear to refer to the village also
called Kanatasake or New Settlement Village located near
the modern city of Geneva, New York, and at that time one
of the major villages of the Seneca Nation. Other claims

have been advanced for Hammondsport in Steuben County and Havana in Schuyler County (Conover 1884, 1). Red Jacket himself is said to have mentioned two other locations. In a speech at Geneva in 1829 he is reported to have told the audience that he had been born near the west arm of Keuka Lake, near what is now Branchport, New York, where he lived with his parents until he was twelve. He then moved to Kanadesaga (Kanataske) and then several years later to Conewagus (or Canawaugus, near Avon, New York) (Cleveland 1873, 450). But in his testimony at the Tommy-Jemmy trial in Buffalo in 1821 Red Jacket said that he had been born at Canoga while his parents were on a fishing trip (Bryant 1879, 370–71). He made a similar statement in a speech at Waterloo, New York, in 1829 and pointed out the exact spot to Judge Garry Sackett of Seneca Falls (Conover 1884, 2–5; Waterloo 1892, 28–30). Lewis Henry Morgan, who researched the Seneca in the 1830s and 1840s, was also told that Red Jacket had been born at Canoga and that the Seneca name of the village was Ga-no-geh, translated as "Oil on the Water" (Morgan 1851, 423, 470). The Canoga location, the most probable site of Red Jacket's birth, is marked by a monument erected by the Waterloo Literary and Historical Society in 1891 (Waterloo 1892).

A small stream flows by the place of Red Jacket's birth and into Cayuga Lake. This stream originates in a spring claimed to have special qualities, "it being the spot where Ha-wen-iu, the Master Spirit, once dropped a tear" (Parker 1943, 525–33). A nineteenth-century historian noted the unusual purity of the water of the Canoga spring and that nitrogen gas rose through the water, making it bubble (Delafield 1850, 408–9, 471–72).

The historian Arthur C. Parker, descended through his father from Seneca ancestors, sought out oral traditions about Red Jacket's family. Parker learned that Red Jacket's mother was named Ah-wey-ne-yohn, translated as "Drooping Flower" or "Blue Flower." Ah-wey-ne-yohn was a Seneca of the Wolf Clan from Kanadesaga (or Kanataske). Red Jacket's father Thadahwahnyeh, was a Cayuga of the Turtle Clan from Skoiyase, near Waterloo, New York (Parker 1952, 3–4; Parker 1943, 528). Among the Iroquois the child's identity follows that of the mother, so Red Jacket was a Seneca of the Wolf Clan. Parker also determined that the site on Keuka Lake, although the location of Red Jacket's birth, was the place where Red Jacket spent his childhood and where his mother is buried. This village was called Ne-do-cio-weh-ah, "Little Vale of Basswoods" (Parker 1943, 524–33; see also Stork 1898, 87–88).

The date of Red Jacket's birth is equally uncertain. McKenney states that Red Jacket was born in 1756 (McKenney 1967, 3). Red Jacket's first major biographer, William L. Stone, and J. Niles Hubbard, whose work closely follows Stone's, both say that Red Jacket was born in 1750 (Stone 1841, 18; Hubbard 1886, 10). The date "1750" however, may be merely a misreading or faulty transcription on the part of Stone or his typesetter, because Stone cites McKenney as his source. Unfortunately, Stone's error has been perpetuated in reference sources.

The most authoritative evidence of the date of Red Jacket's birth comes from Red Jacket himself in testimony given at the Tommy Jemmy trial in 1821. Asked his age, Red Jacket replied that he did not know but that his mother had told him that he was just big enough to crawl around on the floor when Fort Niagara was taken by the British (Bryant 1879, 370–71). Because Sir William Johnson captured Fort Niagara from the French in July 1759, Red Jacket was probably born sometime in 1758.

Red Jacket has been described as a person of obscure birth who obtained high rank through his own efforts, and he has been described as springing from an Indian aristocracy. Thomas Proctor, who met him in 1791, described him as "the great prince of the turtle tribe" (*ASPIA* 1:155, 169). A famous poem about Red Jacket, written by Fitz-Green Hallack in 1829, portrays Red Jacket as an hereditary chief of the Tuscarora, a claim that misidentifies Red Jacket's tribe and misunderstands the political system of the Iroquois.

Red Jacket was a chief, but his exact rank remains a mystery. There are fifty "league chiefs," sometimes called "sachems" in the Iroquois Confederacy. Each of these fifty descend within a particular tribe and clan. Red Jacket's tribe, the Senecas, have eight league chiefs, and one of these belongs to Red Jacket's Wolf Clan. In addition, "pine tree chiefs" can be created to assist in the business of the tribe and the confederacy and, when needed, "war chiefs" as well. None of these ranks is hereditary (Snow 1994, 65, 129–30; Parker 1916a, 41–42).

Because the clan identity of the son follows that of the mother, a son could not follow his father as a league chief. A nephew could follow an uncle if they shared a common clan identity through the female line. It was the women of the tribe and clan who determined the succession. Further, it was the women of a particular lineage who made the decision. The title of a league chief could not have been passed from a father to son. Clan identity came from the mother. Red Jacket's father was a Turtle, but his mother was a Wolf, and, therefore, Red Jacket was of the Wolf Clan. Horatio Hale, a nineteenth-century student of Iroquois customs and language, wrote that rank was hereditary in certain families, and that Red Jacket's family did not belong to that class (BHS 1885, 72). Thomas Morris, who negotiated with Red Jacket in the 1790s, also believed that Red Jacket was of low birth and, thus, ineligible to become a sachem (Morris, "Pioneer Settlements," 9, in O'Reilly Collection). Hale and Morris are contradicted by Ely S. Parker (1828–1895), himself a league chief, who denied that families could be "aristocratic" because titles belonged to the clan and not to any one family (BHS 1885, 67). But was Red Jacket from an obscure family? His father is almost unknown and was Cayuga rather than Seneca, but Red Jacket's status derived from the female line. Strong refers to Red Jacket's grandmother as a "woman of influence" among the chiefs (Strong 1863, 6). Governor Blacksnake stated that Red Jacket's mother was a sister of his own mother (Draper Manuscripts, 4-S-74). Blacksnake's mother was the sister (or half-sister) of Cornplanter (1730s–1836) and Handsome Lake (1735–1815) (Abler 1989, 2–3, 19). Red Jacket was, therefore, the nephew, and of the same clan as Cornplanter and Handsome Lake and, thus, closely related to persons of considerable stature and influence.

Whatever Red Jacket's inherited status, he took an early interest in political affairs. According to Nathaniel Strong, at an age when other children were hunting squirrels or playing ball, Red Jacket spent his time attending councils and listening carefully to the proceedings. Red Jacket soon became a favorite of the council and when he was strong enough, he was chosen to carry messages to the other parts of the Seneca Nation and to neighboring tribes. In an oral and politically sophisticated culture the responsibility of accurately transmitting the words spoken in council was an important trust (Strong 1863, 4–5). McKenney states that Red Jacket became a "runner" at the age of seventeen (McKenney 1967, 4). Runners not only had to have good memories but considerable physical ability. Lewis Henry Morgan was told that Iroquois runners could deliver messages from Buffalo to Albany in an incredible three days (Morgan 1851, 441–42).

Red Jacket had political ambitions. Among the Iroquois, orators were esteemed, and Red Jacket wanted to become an orator. According to a story told by Red Jacket to Thomas Maxwell, Red Jacket was present at a council and heard the noted Mingo (the Mingos were Iroquois people who lived in the Ohio country) orator Logan (ca. 1725–1780) speak. Red Jacket was so impressed by Logan's manner and delivery that he resolved to attain the same standard of eloquence and practiced at "playing Logan" (Turner 1851, 487–88). Red Jacket was not yet known as Red Jacket. He was given an infant name, now forgotten, at his birth, and at the age of ten was given a new name, Otetiani, meaning "Always Ready" (Parker 1952, 10; Hubbard 1886, 77–78, 110–11; BHS 1885, 77–78, 110–11). It is possible that the name was selected to recognize the services of the young Red Jacket to the chiefs in council.

Red Jacket was just beginning to crawl when Fort Niagara was taken by the British in 1759. Possibly he was aware of the fighting between the Seneca and the British in 1763 during the Pontiac War, when Seneca warriors attacked and captured British posts at Venango, Le Bouef, and Presqu'Isle in Pennsylvania, and destroyed two British detachments from Fort Niagara at Devil's Hole near Niagara Falls (Wallace 1972, 114–17). After the end of the Seven Years War, the Proclamation Line of October 1763 set an eastern boundary between the lands of the Iroquois and those of the British colonists. The proclamation did not stop white colonists from moving into Kentucky and into the Ohio Country. The Iroquois relinquished their claim to Kentucky at the Treaty of Fort Stanwix in 1768, but Seneca warriors joined with the western tribes to defend the Ohio country in Lord Dunmore's War in 1774. It was during this decade of conflict that the family of Chief Logan, the orator who had so impressed the young Red Jacket, was massacred by whites (Wallace 1969, 114–17, 121–25).

The years of Red Jacket's childhood and early adolescence were troubled times, but the lands of the Senecas, although the British posts at Niagara, Venango, Le Bouef, and Presqu'Isle encroached on the western portions of their territory, were still far beyond the limits of white settlement. In the next decade, 1775–1784, the Six Nations were drawn into the conflict between rebel colonials, loyalist colonials, and Britain. Farmer's Brother, an important Seneca chief, would later describe that conflict as "a great tumult and commotion, like a raging whirlwind which tears up the trees, and tosses to and fro the leaves, so that no one knows from whence they came and where they will fall" (*Monthly Anthology*, Mar. 1809, 158). It was within this whirlwind that Red Jacket's voice was first heard in the councils of the Six Nations.

2

From the Revolution
to Fort Stanwix, 1775–1784

A little more than one decade after the defeat of the French in 1763, a new conflict arose in North America, this time between the British and their rebellious colonies. Both sides courted the Iroquois. The Americans urged the Six Nations to remain neutral while the British reminded them of their earlier agreements and asked them to join in quelling the rebellion. The Iroquois Confederacy was divided. The Mohawks, particularly Joseph Brant, supported the British. The Oneida and Tuscarora inclined toward the Americans. The Onondaga, Cayuga, and Seneca, furthest removed from the dispute, were initially inclined to remain neutral.

Governor Blacksnake recalled many years later that Red Jacket had spoken for the Six Nations at councils held at Fort Pitt and Albany in 1775 and 1776 where he assured the Americans of the intention of the Six Nations to "keep hands down for peace with all sides" (Abler 1989, 47–56; 1989; Thwaites and Kellogg 1908, 159–67). William Jones, a Seneca, although born after the Revolution, told J. Niles Hubbard that Red Jacket had voiced his opposition to war: "This quarrel does not belong to us, and it is best for us to take no part in it; we need not waste our blood to have it settled. If they fight us, we will fight them, but if they leave us alone, we better keep still" (Hubbard 1886, 45).

Despite appeals from the British the Seneca remained neutral through the first two years of the war. In June 1777 Colonel John Butler, the British agent at Niagara, tried to enlist the support of the Six Nations for the planned invasion of New York from the British post at Oswego on Lake Ontario. Butler held his council at Irondequoit Bay, near the mouth of the Genesee River at Lake Ontario, in July. Cornplanter and Old Smoke, a Seneca war chief, again repeated the desire of the Seneca to remain neutral. This time, however, the British arguments and numerous gifts to the assembled Indians prevailed, and after two weeks of meetings, the assembled Indians of the Six Nations agreed to aid the British cause (Graymont 1972, 118–23; Seaver 1990, 49–51).

Although Red Jacket had earlier spoken for peace, his nation had chosen war. At Oswego, Cornplanter and Old Smoke were named war chiefs, and several "active young men," including Red Jacket and his cousin Blacksnake, were named war captains (Draper Manuscripts, 4-S-20). Red Jacket, or Otetiani as he was still called, would prove a very reluctant warrior.

Directly after the Oswego council, the Seneca joined the British who were besieging Fort Stanwix. Red Jacket was part of a force sent to stop the American force under General Nicholas Herkimer that was marching to the relief of Stanwix. The two forces clashed at the Battle of Oriskany on August 6, 1777. At the opening volley, Red Jacket, with three other warriors, fled and returned to the Genesee country. Because Red Jacket was young and it was his first battle, nothing was done or said to him (Draper Manuscripts, 4-S-24).

In June and July 1778 Red Jacket was part of the expedition to the Wyoming Valley in Pennsylvania. This time he participated in the battle with the American militia on July 3, but kept behind the main Indian body at "long shooting distance" of the fighting and killed no one (Draper Manuscripts, 4-S-29). In November 1778 he joined the expedition to attack Cherry Valley but turned back at Tioga, complaining of the lateness of the season (Draper Manuscripts, 4-S-31).

In 1777 and 1778 combined Iroquois, British, and Loyalist forces attacked the frontiers of New York and Pennsylvania. In the summer of 1779 the Americans took the war to the heart of the Iroquois country in the Sullivan-Clinton campaign. The aim was to burn the Indian villages and crops. At the Battle of Newtown, east of the present city of Elmira, on August 29, 1779, the British and Indian positions were shelled by the American artillery, and Red Jacket was said to be among the first to run. There was little the Indians or their British allies could do but try to harry and ambush the invading American column.

It was during this campaign that Red Jacket received the name "Cow Killer." The story, as told by Joseph Brant to Thomas Morris, was that Red Jacket, after having urged the Senecas to attack the invaders, not only kept out of harm's way but killed some of his neighbor's cows to feed his own family (Morris, Pioneer Settlements, 8–9 in O'Reilly Collection; Wallace 1972, 25–26). In a more elaborate version of the story Red Jacket and another warrior kill a cow. Red Jacket wipes the blood on his hatchet and returns to camp claiming that he has killed an American. His companion, amused by Red Jacket's claim, tells what really happened, much to the discomfort of Red Jacket (Draper Manuscripts, 4-S-36-37; Abler 1989, 109; Kelsay 1984, 541; Stone 1838, 2:419; Wallace 1972, 25–26). In British reports of Indian Councils in the 1790s, Red Jacket is commonly referred to as Cow Killer (Simcoe 1923, 1: 220, 224, 256). The story circulated for the remainder of Red Jacket's life.

On another occasion Cornplanter attempted to stop Red Jacket from retreating from the advancing American forces. Frustrated by Red Jacket, Cornplanter turned to Red Jacket's wife, saying, "Leave that man—he is a coward" (McKenney 1967, 4; Stone 1841, 22; Hubbard 1886, 49). In another version of the story related by Jasper Parrish, it was Farmer's Brother who told Red Jacket's wife "not to bear sons of which he was the father, for they would be inheritors of his cowardice" (Turner 1851, 468).

Joseph Brant later told Peter B. Porter that after the battle of Newtown, Red Jacket had held private councils with the younger warriors to attempt to persuade them to ask for peace with the Americans. Red Jacket and his party sent a runner to American General Sullivan to begin negotiations. Brant heard of the attempt and secretly sent two warriors, who killed a man with a flag of truce who had been sent by the Americans in response to Red Jacket's overtures (Stone 1838, 2:35; Stone 1841, 21–22). The authenticity of this story is very doubtful. Isabel Kelsay in her biography of Joseph Brant states that if any such overture was intended, word of it never reached Sullivan (Kelsay 1984, 264).

The stories of Red Jacket's cowardice came from Red Jacket's political rivals, Joseph Brant and Cornplanter. It is possible that they are overdrawn. Even allowing for bias, however, it seems clear that Red Jacket was no warrior. His later positions of leadership among the Seneca and the Six Nations reflect his political and oratorical skills, not his military merit. In 1850 the elderly Governor Blacksnake told many stories of Red Jacket's cowardice in the American Revolution, yet smiled when he did so. He had Red Jacket's portrait in his room and, according to Draper, appeared to have more reverence for Red Jacket than for any other Indian (Draper Manuscripts, 4-S-75; Graymont 1972, 215–16).

The destruction of the Iroquois villages and crops in the summer of 1779 caused many Iroquois to seek refuge near the British fort at Niagara. In 1780 many of these refugees from several tribes began to build new homes along Buffalo Creek near the present city of Buffalo, New York. For the remainder of his life, except for a brief exile at Tonawanda, Red Jacket would be closely identified with Buffalo Creek.

The power of the Six Nations was not destroyed by the Sullivan-Clinton expedition. The British, Loyalist, and Indian forces continued their raids along the New York frontier in 1780, 1781, and into 1782. Red Jacket took part in an attack at Schoharie in October 1780 and acquitted himself well. With the surrender of Cornwallis at Yorktown in October 1781, however, the British effort to end the rebellion was all but concluded. Hostilities between the two sides effectively ended with the Preliminary Articles of Peace in November 1782 and were finalized in the Treaty of Paris in 1783.

The Treaty of Paris drew boundaries between the United States and the British possessions in Canada. The treaty, though, did not address the fate of Britain's Indian allies, who were now within the boundaries of the land conceded to the United States. Many of the Iroquois, particularly the members of the Mohawk Nation, fled into Canada, settling at Tyendinaga or Deseronto, on the Bay of Quinte on the north side of Lake Ontario and along the Grand River. Other Iroquois, including most of the Seneca, remained for a time on their old lands (Snow 1994, 152).

Over the next thirty years the diplomacy of the Six Nations and the Seneca Nation was intertwined with the conflict between the British and the United States. At stake was the future control of the Ohio country. At a grand council of the Indian nations held at Au Glaze, at the juncture of the Auglaze and Maumee Rivers in Ohio during September and October 1792, Red Jacket reviewed the history of the American Revolution. At first, the king told them that he would soon chastise his unruly children. The Americans, on their part, had desired that the Six Nations remain out of the quarrel. But then the king desired that the Six Nations would take his part. In the end the king was defeated, made his own peace, and left the Seneca to reach their own accommodation with the new United States. "Our Father [the king] then desired us to speak to the Americans for as advantageous a peace as we could get for ourselves. We have been trying to do so in the best manner we could" (Simcoe 1923, 1:222).

The stance of the young United States toward the Mohawks, Onondagas, Cayugas, and Senecas was harsh. They were to be treated as the defeated enemy. At Fort Stanwix in October 1784 the commissioners appointed by the United States berated the Indians, telling them they were a subdued people. The treaty, signed October 22, 1784, declared peace and received the Senecas, Mohawks, Onondagas, and Cayugas into the protection of the United States. The United States considered the other two nations of the Iroquois Confederacy, the Oneida and Tuscarora, as allies. Their treatment, however, was little better than that of the defeated nations (Campisi 1988, 49–57; Wallace 1972, 149–52).

The major provision of the treaty, other than the declaration of peace, was to set the western boundaries of the Six Nations. In New York the boundary was a line drawn from the mouth of Buffalo Creek to the Pennsylvania border. This line not only cut off Seneca lands in the western part of what is now New York State but also denied the Iroquois claims to the vast Ohio country. Although the boundary lines were written down in the treaty document, the legitimacy of the treaty and the land cessions were not accepted by the Six Nations. A council of the Six Nations held at Buffalo after the negotiations at Fort Stanwix refused to ratify the treaty (Graymont 1972, 284).

General Lafayette was at the Treaty of Fort Stanwix. In 1825, during his tour of the United States, Lafayette met Red Jacket in Buffalo. Lafayette asked whether Red Jacket remembered the young warrior who had spoken against the proposed treaty and wanted to go on fighting. In a dramatic gesture Red Jacket said, "He is before you" (Stone 1841, 358). Although this meeting of old enemies is appropriately dramatic, it is not certain that Red Jacket was even at Fort Stanwix (Draper Manuscripts, 4-S-75; Graymont 1972, 275–76). In his later years Red Jacket made much of his association with George Washington, and he may have considered that the chance to link his name with that of the famous General Lafayette was too good to pass up.

Red Jacket's call for a continuation of the war in 1784 and the report that he did so again at a council near Detroit in December 1786 (Stone 1841, 26–27; Eckert 1992, 294–302) seem out of character. In later years Red Jacket consistently spoke for peace and negotiation. His reported belligerent stance in the late 1780s may reflect an earlier belief that military resistance was possible or may derive from his role as a speaker for the Seneca rather than from his personal position.

The Six Nations in council refused to ratify the Treaty of Fort Stanwix (Graymont 1972, 284), but the United States persisted in treating it as binding. The Indians, however, continued to question the legitimacy of the agreement. The relationship between the Six Nations and the United States would not be resolved until the Treaty of Canandaigua in 1794.

Although Red Jacket did not gain fame as a warrior, his diplomatic services as a runner attracted the favorable attention of the British at Fort Niagara. In recognition, British officers presented him with a red jacket, which he took pride in wearing. From this time onward he was commonly known to the whites as "Red Jacket." At the Treaty of Canandaigua in 1794 the American commissioner, Timothy Pickering, presented him with another coat "to perpetuate the name to which he was so much attached" (McKenney 1976, 4).

Interviewed in the 1850s, Governor Blacksnake remembered Red Jacket and Cornplanter as the principal leaders of
the Seneca at the negotiations at the beginning of the
Revolution. In 1776, however, Red Jacket was probably no
more than eighteen and certainly no older than twenty-six
years of age. Although Red Jacket may have participated in
those meetings, there is reason to be skeptical that Red
Jacket was this prominent in the 1770s (Abler 1989, 38). Red
Jacket's participation in councils, however, often rested on
his skills as an orator. Although the young Red Jacket may
not have had great standing as a political leader in the 1770s,
he was already a runner and may have been recognized as
a talented speaker.

About this time Red Jacket received a new name, usually
transliterated as Sagoyewatha, and variously translated as
"Keeper Awake" or "He Who Keeps Them Awake" (BHS
1885, 71). Lewis Henry Morgan believed that the name referred to Red Jacket's powers of eloquence, and Nathaniel
Strong, a native speaker of the Seneca language, stated that
the name implied magical powers (Morgan 1851, 90; Strong,
1863, 3). Wallace Chafe, the author of a modern dictionary
of the Seneca language, gives the modern preferred translit-
eration as Shagóye:wa:tha? He Wakes Them Up Early." Chafe
is skeptical of Morgan's assertion that the name is a reference
to Red Jacket's oratory (Chafe 1967, 87; and personal communications with author 1997).

In 1821, at the trial of Tommy-Jemmy in Buffalo, Red
Jacket was one of those giving testimony. One of the councils asked Red Jacket what his rank was. Red Jacket replied,
"Look at the papers which the white people keep most
carefully," (meaning the treaties ceding their lands) they will
tell you what I am!" (Stone 1841, 320).

It was a rhetorical flourish worthy of the famous orator
because it says nothing about his actual status. Red Jacket's

two major biographers, William L. Stone and J. Niles Hubbard, both identify Red Jacket as a sachem and repeat a story that Stone derived from a conversation with Thomas Morris about Red Jacket scheming to be made a chief (Stone 1838, 2:415–16; 1841 25–26; Hubbard 1886, 58–59). The story in Morris's own hand, in a manuscript account written in 1844, prepared at the request of Rochester historian Henry O'Reilly is now preserved in the New-York Historical Society.

Morris repeats an anecdote "generally believed to be correct" that Red Jacket was ineligible to become a sachem because of his humble birth. Red Jacket, therefore, told the Indians that he had a dream that the Great Spirit had told him that they would never prosper until they made him a sachem. Alhough the Iroquois placed great importance on dreams, they at first discounted Red Jacket's claim. Red Jacket persisted in attributing all the misfortunes of the Indians to their failure to comply with the will of the Great Spirit. Finally, Red Jacket secured the position of sachem (Morris, Pioneer Settlements, 9, in O'Reilly Collection).

When Hubbard used the story in his 1886 biography, he stated that this allegation had been denied by some and speculates that Joseph Brant, Red Jacket's political enemy, may have spread the story (Hubbard 1886, 59). Thomas Morris's account must be given considerable weight. Morris, as the agent of his father, the land speculator and financier William Morris, spent considerable time in and near the Seneca country from 1791 to 1797, preparing to negotiate the purchase of the western New York lands from the Seneca. He knew Red Jacket, Cornplanter, Brant, Jasper Parrish, and the other important figures of the 1790s. Red Jacket and Morris clashed at the Treaty of Big Tree in 1797, and although Morris was obviously impressed by Red Jacket, he is also the source of several uncomplimentary stories about Red Jacket that were subsequently publicized by William T.

Stone, who was an admirer of Joseph Brant. Was he correct, however, in asserting that Red Jacket had been made a league chief?

In the *League of the Ho-Dé-No-Sau-Nee Iroquois,* Lewis Henry Morgan clearly distinguished between the office of sachem and that of chief and comments that Red Jacket was never able to elevate himself higher than a chief and, in a possible reference to the story told by Morris and Stone, noted that Red Jacket may have "practiced on the superstitious fears of his people" to attain even this rank (Morgan 1851, 103).

Stone's books on Brant and Red Jacket, which appeared at the time when Lewis Henry Morgan was first becoming interested in the Iroquois, are based almost exclusively on Euroamerican accounts of the Iroquois. Morgan, in contrast, was primarily interested in Iroquois accounts and in the *League of the Ho-Dé-No-Sau-Nee Iroquois,* based his account of the Iroquois polity on information derived from Iroquois informants, particularly the young Ely S. Parker.

Fortunately, Parker's direct testimony backs up the account related by Morgan. In 1884, at the time of Red Jacket's reburial in Forest Lawn Cemetery in Buffalo, Parker specifically stated that Red Jacket was never a sachem or league officer although Parker also noted that Red Jacket "used every means which his wisdom and cunning could devise to make himself appear not only the foremost man of his tribe but of the League." Parker goes on to suggest that it was not the circumstances of his birth, but his character flaws, that made Red Jacket ineligible for league office (BHS 1885, 68–69). This last view contradicts the implication of Morris's and Stone's accounts and Horatio Hale's categorical statement that Red Jacket was ineligible because his family did not belong to the class from which league chiefs were chosen (BHS 1885, 72).

Nathaniel T. Strong provides an alternative account of Red Jacket gaining the favor of the chiefs and sachems through his service to them and gaining rank in part through the influence of his grandmother, a woman of influence. Strong states that Red Jacket was created a "sachem of the second class" with the name of Go yo so doh or "Crosses Standing Perpendicular" but, against the custom and rules of the Confederation, never assumed the name although he did hold the office (Strong, 1863, 6–7).

These sachems of the second class may be the people described by Lewis Henry Morgan as "subsachems." These individuals, distinct from pine tree chiefs, acted as aids to sachems. A subsachem was "raised up at the same time with his superior, with the same forms and ceremonies, and received the name or title which was created simultaneously with that of the sachemship." In a later work Morgan states that these assistant sachems (called "Braces in the Long House") were the likely successors of their sachems (Morgan 1851, 68–69; Schoolcraft 1847, 495; Morgan 1965, 31).

The evidence is contradictory. Red Jacket became a man of considerable importance among the Seneca and in the councils of the Six Nations. It seems likely that he was a pine tree chief raised up by his own skills, rather than a league chief or sachem although he may have at one time held the office of subsachem. In the end Red Jacket's exact political rank, whether pine tree chief, sachem, or subsachem, is not very important. He was first and last an orator and a diplomat, and in the forty years between 1790 and 1830 it was the voice of Red Jacket that most frequently spoke for the Seneca Nation.

3

An Uneasy Peace, 1784–1790

The destruction of the Iroquois villages and crops by the Sullivan-Clinton expedition in 1779 forced many of the Iroquois to seek refuge near British-held Fort Niagara. In 1780 many of the Indian refugees began building new homes along Buffalo Creek, which runs from Lake Erie in what is now the City of Buffalo and extends eastward through what is now West Seneca. The geographical center of the Seneca nation was moving westward from the Finger Lakes and Genesee Valley to the Niagara Frontier and western New York. Senecas were the largest portion of the Indians living at Buffalo Creek, but many Cayugas, Onondagas, and Munsees also moved there.

After the close of the Revolution, many members of the Six Nations moved to Canada where they settled along the Grand River on the Haldimand Grant, a tract of land purchased by the British government and presented to their faithful allies. A second group of Mohawks settled at Tyendinaga on the Bay of Quinte, along the north shore of Lake Ontario (Kelsay 1984, 363; Allen 1992, 58–59). The old organization of the long house with the Mohawks guarding the eastern door and the Senecas guarding the western door was in disarray. Many of the Mohawks were now on the Grand River, and with them were Iroquois from all the other tribes of the Six Nations (Kelsay 1984, 370).

In New York many Oneida, Onondaga, and Cayuga continued to live in their old homes, and the Seneca continued to inhabit their older villages in the Genesee Valley, but the newer villages in the western part of the state were growing in importance. The settlements along Buffalo and Cayuga Creeks in what is now Erie County included villages of Seneca, Onondaga, Cayuga, and Munsees.

The Six Nations had been divided in the Revolution, the Mohawk, Onondaga, Cayuga, and Seneca, with some exceptions, siding with the British, and the Oneida and Tuscarora, again with some exceptions, siding with the Americans. Now there was a new political reality. The Confederacy was split between those living within the boundaries claimed by the United States and those living in British Canada. In Canada the Mohawk chief, Joseph Brant (1743–1807), became the major voice in the negotiations of the 1780s and 1790s. In the United States leadership often came from the Seneca, with Cornplanter, Farmer's Brother, and, increasingly, Red Jacket speaking for the Iroquois.

The Treaty of Fort Stanwix, signed October 22, 1784, secured the Six Nations in the "peaceful possession" of their lands in New York and Pennsylvania. Possession, however, lasted only until the Iroquois, or the individual tribes, could be convinced to sell those lands. Immediately after the treaty was signed, commissioners from Pennsylvania met with Indians and convinced them to sell their lands in Pennsylvania, telling them in effect that they had no alternative to selling. The reluctant Indians signed the deed on October 23, selling most of northwest Pennsylvania for four thousand dollars in goods (Graymont 1972, 282–83). The State of New York began the purchase of the Six Nations' lands with the acquisition of a large tract of Oneida and Tuscarora lands on June 28, 1785. Most of the remaining Oneida lands were "ceded" in September 1788 (Campisi 1988, 56–60; O'Reilly 1838, 107).

Most of the Seneca lands from Seneca Lake westward were within territory claimed by both New York State and Massachusetts. The two states came to an amicable settlement of their differences at the Treaty of Hartford on December 16, 1785. Massachusetts ceded to New York the jurisdiction over the disputed lands while New York ceded the ownership to Massachusetts. Because the Treaty of Fort Stanwix secured the Indians in the possession of these same lands, the agreement gave Massachusetts the "preemptive right" to purchase the lands when and if the Indians were willing to sell. The preemption line ran north-south from the Pennsylvania border to Lake Ontario, passing just west of Seneca Lake and the modern city of Geneva, New York, and terminating west of Sodus Bay on Lake Ontario. In 1787 Massachusetts sold the preemptive right to Oliver Phelps and Nathaniel Gorham (Turner 1851, 105–6).

New York State forbade the private purchase of Indian land, but in 1787 the New York Genesee Land Company was formed. Rather than attempt an outright purchase, the company negotiated the "lease" of all of the Six Nations' land in New York, with the exception of reservations of unstated size, for an annual rent of two thousand dollars. The "lease" not only circumvented New York State law but also negated the interests of Phelps and Gorham, who had the sole right to purchase the lands west of the preemption line. The lease was to run for 999 years. The State of New York voided the lease but not without considerable trouble and several meetings with the Indians (O'Reilly 1838, 106–22)

In July 1788 Oliver Phelps traveled to Canandaigua. The Senecas were prepared to sell land but desired to make the Genesee River the eastern boundary of their territory. The purchasers also demanded, and after several days received, a parcel of land west of the Genesee River, running from Avon to Lake Ontario.

Red Jacket is said to have made a great speech on this occasion, enumerating the wrongs suffered by the Indians at the hands of the white men. The whites present began to fear for their lives, but Farmer's Brother interposed and was able to prevent violence (O'Reilly 1838, 132–33; Thatcher 1840, 2:274–75). The authenticity of this event is doubtful.

For about 2,500,000 acres the Senecas were to be paid five thousand dollars and an annual annuity of five hundred dollars. That, at least, was Phelps and Gorham's version of the agreement. At Tioga Point (Athens, Pennsylvania) on November 21, 1790, Red Jacket reviewed the terms of the agreement. Red Jacket told Pickering that the agreed upon purchase price was ten thousand dollars. "When we discovered the fraud," said Red Jacket, "we had a mind to apply to Congress, to see if the matter could not be rectified: for, when we took the money and shared it . . . we had but about a dollar a piece for all that country. . . . At the time of the treaty, twenty broaches would not buy half a loaf of bread, so that when we returned home, we had not a bright spot of silver about us" (ASPIA 1:214–15).

———

They were also dissatisfied with the boundary. They told Pickering in 1792 that they understood that the line west of the Genesee River at Canawaugus (near Avon, New York) was only to go to a certain spring but had accepted a figure citing the distance as twelve miles, which marked off a much bigger tract than they had planned to sell. Pickering used the opportunity to recommend that their children be instructed in reading and writing that they might not be imposed upon in the future. Pickering also used the occasion to drive a wedge between the New York Iroquois and the British by reminding them that they had acted on the advice of their "British friends" from Niagara. Red Jacket responded by saying that they knew Brant had been bribed. Pickering did not mention that the American missionary Samuel Kirkland had also advised the Indians at the Phelps-Gorham purchase (Pickering to Israel Chapin, Ap. 29, 1792, Pickering Papers, 62–027, 027A).

The lands east of the Genesee were gone. Red Jacket and Farmer's Brother reviewed their grievances with Timothy Pickering in November 1790, and Cornplanter did the same with President Washington at Philadelphia in December 1790. The United States government did investigate the complaints and collected statements from the white men present at the treaty who confirmed the Phelps and Gorham version (ASPIA 1:206–15). Pickering concluded that the Senecas were mistaken in their belief about the terms of the treaty but also that the Seneca had surely been abused. In a letter to Israel Chapin on April 29, 1792, after a council with Red Jacket and others, Pickering ended by expressing his indignation on the "impositions perpetually practiced in the purchase of Indian lands" (Pickering to Chapin, Pickering Papers, 62-027, 27A).

By the terms of the Treaty of Fort Stanwix in 1784 the Six Nations yielded to the United States all claims to the Ohio country west of New York and Pennsylvania. This land included what is now the state of Ohio and an undefined (at least for the Americans) amount of territory west of that state in Indiana and Michigan. This cessation was repeated at the Treaty of Fort Harmar on January 9, 1789, although on this occasion the Six Nations were also given three thousand dollars in goods. In both cases the Six Nations felt that the treaties had been forced upon them.

The Six Nations were closely involved in the diplomacy with the Indian tribes in the Ohio country until after the War of 1812. They continued to claim authority over several of the tribes in the Ohio country although how much actual power the Confederacy had in the region is difficult to determine. In the following speech, unfortunately undated, Red Jacket sarcastically berates the "Quatoghies" (possibly meaning the Wyandots) and the Lenapees (Delawares) for presuming to light a council fire.

Have the Quatoghies forgotten themselves? Or do they suppose we have forgotten them? Who gave you the right in the west or the east to light the general council fire? You must have fallen asleep, and dreamt that the Six Nations were dead! Who permitted you to escape from the lower country? Had you any heart left to speak a word for yourselves? Remember how you hung on by the bushes. You had not even a place to land on. . . .

As for you, my nephews, he continued, turning to the Lenapees, or Delawares, it is fit you should let another light your fire. . . . Could you hunt or plant without our leave? Could you sell a foot of land? Did not the voice of the Long House cry, go, and you went? Had you any power at all? Fit act indeed for you to give in to our wandering brothers— you, from whom we took the war-club and put on petticoats. (Schoolcraft 1847, 182–83)

In late 1786 a council of the western nations was held near the mouth of the Detroit River attended by the Hurons, Ottawas, Shawnees, Chippewas, Delawares, Pottawattamies, Wabash Confederates, and the Six Nations. The issue was to define the common boundaries of the Indian country. Red Jacket is reported to have delivered a great speech, saying that unless the United States agreed to the boundary lines, the Indian nations should make common cause and continue the war (Stone 1841, 27). In Isabel Kelsay's biography of Joseph Brant, she credits Brant with leading the delegation of the Six Nations and for speaking forcibly for unity among the Indian nations (1984, 403–4). Kelsay does not mention Red Jacket.

Knowledge of Red Jacket's role in the Revolution and subsequent events up to the Livingston leases in 1787 is based on later recollections. The first contemporary documentation of Red Jacket may be his signature on the Livingston lease in 1787. He signed the Phelps-Gorham sale, but his role in the sale appears to have been minor. His voice, from 1775 to 1788, was heard in the councils of the Six Nations. Beginning in 1790, his voice would be clearly heard in the councils with the British and the Americans, and his words were recorded and preserved in the records of those councils. It is in the 1790s, the period of Red Jacket's greatest influence, that the relations between the United States and the Iroquois nations in New York were reexamined and renegotiated, resulting in a relationship based on a mutually agreed upon treaty—rather than the imposed victor's settlement of 1784.

4

Tioga Point to the Canandaigua Treaty, 1790–1794

In 1784 the United States treated the Senecas, Mohawks, Onondagas, and Cayugas as defeated enemies. The Treaty of Fort Stanwix had stripped the Iroquois of the lands that they claimed in the Erie triangle and the Ohio country. Although the western boundary set at Stanwix was reconfirmed at the Treaty of Fort Harmar in 1789, neither treaty was accepted as legitimate by most of the Six Nations. The Iroquois, and particularly the Senecas in western New York, continued to be closely interested in affairs in the Ohio country and would continue to assert their claims of authority in that region. In addition, some Senecas moved to the Sandusky River in northwest Ohio in the late 1780s (Tanner 1987, 89).

By 1790 the attitude of the United States government toward the Indians in New York had shifted. The movement of Americans across the Ohio River into the old northwest was being stoutly resisted by the Indian nations in the region, who were insisting on the Ohio River as the boundary line. Relations with the western Indian nations and military action against them took much of the attention and resources of the newly formed United States. In the mix of war and diplomacy the United States again looked toward the Indian Nations of New York, in part to assure Iroquois

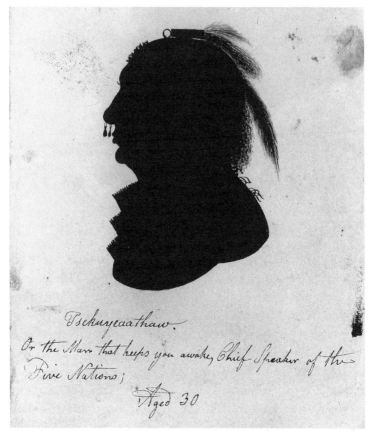

Tschuryeaathaw.

Or the Man that keeps you awake, Chief Speaker of the
Five Nations;
                        Aged 30

Red Jacket, 1790, from the Perot Silhouette Collection.
Courtesy of the Historical Society of Pennsylvania.

neutrality and partly in hopes that the Iroquois would use
their authority and influence in the Ohio country to bring
about a negotiated settlement to the difficulties between the
two sides. It was in the three-way negotiations between the
United States, the New York Indians, and the Western Indians that Red Jacket rose to prominence as a diplomat and
as one of the principal speakers for the Senecas.

The Senecas had their own concerns, including the safety of their people. The increasing proximity of the whites in northwestern Pennsylvania along the southern border of the Iroquois led to a series of violent incidents in which whites were frequently the aggressors. On June 27, 1790, white men murdered two Senecas who had come to Pine Creek in north central Pennsylvania to trade. News of the murders reached the Supreme Executive Council of the State of Pennsylvania, which on July 9 posted an eight hundred dollar reward for the capture of the murderers and wrote to the Seneca Nation, assuring them of their desire for justice and continued peace (Pennsylvania 1853, 396–99). A copy of the letter reached the Senecas at Buffalo Creek, who responded on August 12, telling the Pennsylvania government that the chain of friendship was rusty, and the Governor of Pennsylvania should come himself to brighten it (Pickering Papers, 61-1).

But the United States government was asserting its right to negotiate with the Indian nations. As this was a federal, not a state, concern, President George Washington appointed Timothy Pickering to conduct the council. Pickering was told to be certain that the Indians understood that "all business between them and any part of the United States is hereafter to be transacted by the General Government" (Pickering Papers, 61-6, 10, 11). Pickering sent word to the Senecas that he would meet with them on October 24. Various delays ensued, and the council did not open until November 15.

The council ranged far beyond the initial purpose of burying the hatchet for the murders at Pine Creek. Pickering explained the position of the United States in great detail and asked the indulgence of the Seneca for any errors in his behavior because it was the first time he had met with them. Farmer's Brother and Red Jacket, on behalf of the Senecas, educated Pickering in the protocol of the diplomacy of the Six Nations and outlined their standing grievances.

The council at Tioga Point marks the emergence of Red Jacket into the consciousness of the United States government. Farmer's Brother and Red Jacket delivered most of the speeches on behalf of the Senecas, and by the end of the council Pickering seems to have regarded Red Jacket as the principal speaker. In a memorandum made at the time Pickering recorded Red Jacket's name as "Saco-que-y-wantau," translated as "Sleeper Wake Up." Pickering was clearly impressed by Red Jacket, describing him as "a man of great ambition" (Pickering Papers, 61-113A). Pickering and Red Jacket would meet several times over the next four years until the signing of the Treaty of Canandaigua in 1794.

Red Jacket's speech of November 23, 1790, contained a history of the arrival of the white men to "this island" (North America), who came in vessels and asked permission to come ashore, looking for a place to "hang their kettles." Then they wanted a piece of land. The Great Spirit, said Red Jacket, had made the land for the Indians for their support, but when the white man came, hunting became more difficult. Then traders came and cheated the Indians. Responding to Pickering's proposal that the Indians should turn to farming, Red Jacket said that whites and Indians must each follow their own ancient rules (Pickering Papers, 61–93). In fact, the Iroquois were an agricultural people with a considerable portion of their diet based on the "three sisters" of corn, beans, and squash, grown by the women, and the products of the hunt. The issue was not whether the Iroquois could or would farm, but whether they would adopt the white man's farming methods and, thus, no longer require the large territory necessary to sustain hunting of deer and other animals (Starna 1988, 31–48).

On his part, Timothy Pickering was impressed by the Seneca. In a letter to George Washington on December 31,

1790, he wrote, "I was an utter stranger to the manners of Indians, and to the proper mode of treating with them. But, Sir, I have found that they are not difficult to please. A man must be destitute of humanity, of honesty, or common sense, who should send them away disgusted. He must want sensibility, if he did not sympathize with them, on their recital of the injuries they have experienced from white men" (Sparks 1853, 358–59).

Red Jacket's November 1790 protest against the Phelps-Gorham treaty ends with a statement that the Indians desire that the "chain of friendship may be brightened with the thirteen states as well as the British" (*ASPIA* 1:214–15). This last statement was a reminder to the Americans that the Iroquois retained their independence and were still part of the diplomacy between the United States and Great Britain. If the United States did not deal fairly with the Iroquois in New York, the Indians would look to their British alliance. It behooved the Americans to keep the Indians of New York as allies, not to drive them into the British camp by ill treatment.

While Farmer's Brother and Red Jacket were traveling to Tioga Point to meet with Timothy Pickering, Cornplanter, Half Town, and Big Tree were already in Philadelphia meeting with the government of Pennsylvania to redress grievances. After their meeting with the Pennsylvanians in October, they remained in Philadelphia to meet with President Washington. In a series of speeches addressed to the president between December 1790 and February 1791 they protested the treatment of the Iroquois from the treaty of Fort Stanwix to the present day. Washington responded by stating that no proof had been found to show that Phelps and Gorham had defrauded the Indians. If the Indians believed this to be the case, the courts were open to hear their claims. Washington,

however, noted that the important object was the security of
the remaining Indian land, and that he pledged to protect
(*ASPIA* 1:140–44).

The American government was concerned with the Indians in the Ohio country. In March 1791 Washington sent
Colonel Thomas Proctor on a mission to the Miami and
Wabash Indians. Proctor was instructed to endeavor to convince Cornplanter and as many other Seneca chiefs as possible to accompany him on his mission to the west (*ASPIA*
1:145–46). Proctor set out from Philadelphia on March 12.
He traveled widely in Seneca country, but the main council
was at Buffalo Creek in April where Farmer's Brother and
Red Jacket—"the great speaker and prince of the Turtle
tribe"—resided. Proctor's description is wrong on two points:
first, in implying that Red Jacket held hereditary rank, and
second, by identifying him with the Turtle Clan. Red Jacket
was of the Wolf Clan.

Red Jacket appears to have been the principal spokesman
during the negotiations of the next several days, although
Proctor also noted that Young King and Fish Carrier sat next
to Red Jacket and advised him.

> Tell him . . . that some of his language is soft, but other parts
> of it are too strong; for the danger that is before us is great,
> and our enemies are drunk; and they will not hear what we
> say, like a man that is sober, and we consider that, whatever
> number of the Six Nations accompany him, he will be in
> some danger with himself, and it is likely we shall not live
> long, when the bad Indians see us. Therefore, as it is a
> business of such a great weight to us, we must take council,
> in order to save ourselves, and him, from falling by their
> hands. Moreover, the Indians are not like white men: for
> they must think a great while. He must therefore attend our
> councils, and look and hear till we shall speak on his busi-
> ness, and to-morrow our head men will meet together, and
> try what can be done. (*ASPIA* 1:157)

The resolution of the matter was left to the Indian women, who agreed to send a delegation, including Red Jacket, to accompany Proctor on his mission. Red Jacket was selected by the women to convey this information to Colonel Proctor (*ASPIA* 1:160). Proctor, however, was blocked in his attempt to travel westward by the refusal of the British authorities to allow him to charter a boat to travel to the proposed council site (*ASPIA* 1:143; Kelsay 1984, 443–45). Red Jacket could scarcely have been disappointed by the failure of the mission. The Senecas were for peace but were more concerned with defending their own lands and people against the increasing pressure of land agents and settlers eager to obtain cheap land.

The United States was now treating the Senecas as potential allies rather than defeated enemies. At Fort Stanwix in 1784 the United States had ignored previous treaty protocol. In 1790 Timothy Pickering was willing to negotiate with the Indians using the traditional forms of Indian diplomacy. Red Jacket, at Tioga Point in November 1790, and again at Painted Post in July 1791, was his teacher. Pickering felt that the Indians should ultimately learn the white man's ways but that change could be gradual. Midway through the council, Red Jacket and Pickering clashed. The issue was the appointment of a gunsmith. Red Jacket had taken Pickering's earlier statements to mean that such a person would be appointed by the Six Nations, and Pickering interrupted Red Jacket to correct him. Red Jacket, angered by the interruption, said, "It won't do to talk much more, perhaps we are deceived in the whole." At the next meeting Pickering said that Red Jacket's accusation of deception was not only an insult to him but to the president. Red Jacket, still angered, said that Pickering had "stopped his mouth" and demonstrated by "striking his mouth with a vehement motion" and, in turn, interrupted and behaved rudely to Pickering. Pickering described Red Jacket's behavior as rude and insulting, but at the end of the council, Red Jacket, his wife, and children, came to Pickering's quarters, and they departed as friends (Pickering Papers, 60-110-17).

One of the observers at the Newtown negotiations in 1791 was the young Thomas Morris. More than fifty years later, in 1844, Morris wrote down his memories of first seeing Red Jacket in action. Morris described Red Jacket as thirty or thirty-five, well-formed and intelligent, the most graceful speaker that Morris had ever known. Red Jacket was quick, witty, and could be sarcastic. At times Timothy Pickering would lose his temper, much to the delight of Red Jacket, who was always ready to take advantage of any slip on the part of his opponent (Morris, Pioneer Sketches, 7–8, in O'Reilly Collection; Francello 1989, 46).

Thomas Morris had good reason to be interested in Red Jacket. As the principal agent of his father, Robert Morris, in the purchase of Seneca lands in New York, Thomas Morris and Red Jacket would meet as adversaries several times in the 1790s. The last occasion would be the 1797 Treaty of Big Tree where Thomas Morris successfully negotiated the purchase of the bulk of Seneca land west of the Genesee River.

At Newtown, Pickering invited prominent chiefs to visit Philadelphia, then the site of the U.S. capital, early in 1792. Interest in securing the aid of the Iroquois in negotiations with the western Indians became even more pressing after the crushing defeat of an American military expedition under the command of General Arthur St. Clair along the Wabash in northeast Indiana in October 1791. The invitation was specifically extended to three Seneca chiefs at Allegany— Cornplanter, New Arrow, and Snake (Governor Black- snake?)—and to Farmer's Brother and other important chiefs at Buffalo Creek. Red Jacket is not mentioned by name. Pickering and the government officials at Philadelphia in- tended to invite a small number of important chiefs, but the delegation that arrived in Philadelphia on March 13, 1792, numbered fifty. The delegation represented the five Iroquois nations living in New York (Seneca, Cayuga, Onondaga, Oneida, and Tuscarora) and the Stockbridge Indians, who lived near the Oneida.

The delegation remained in Philadelphia for more than one month. Washington addressed them on March 23 and presented them with a white belt of wampum, representing his desire for peace. Over the next month, the delegation met again with Washington, with Timothy Pickering, and with the governor of Pennsylvania. Red Jacket appears to have been the principal speaker on these occasions. The United States provided an annuity of fifteen hundred dollars to be shared among the New York Indians (*ASPIA* 1: 225–33).

It was undoubtedly on this visit to Philadelphia that Red Jacket received a large silver medal from George Washington. In later years Red Jacket was very proud of this medal and of his direct association with George Washington. Washington, despite being the commander of the American armies during the Revolutionary War who sent the Sullivan and Clinton expeditions to destroy the Iroquois towns, has an honored place among traditional Iroquois (Parker 1913, 66).

Both the British and the United States gave "peace medals" to their prominent Indian leaders. The design adopted in 1792 was an oval of silver with an engraved picture of President Washington and an Indian. The medal came in three sizes, with the larger going to the more important chiefs. Red Jacket received one of the largest size. On the medal Washington, in uniform, stands to the right and gestures toward an Indian on the left, who is also standing and smoking a peace pipe. A house and a man plowing are seen in the background. The Indian's tomahawk has dropped to the ground at his feet, although Washington retains his sword at his side. The message is of peace and friendship with the suggestion that the Indian adopt the white man's ways of farming. The fact that the Indian had dropped his tomahawk

Red Jacket's Washington Peace Medal, 1792.
Courtesy of the Buffalo and Erie County Historical Society.

but Washington still wears a sword could not have been
overlooked by the recipients. Beneath the scene is inscribed
"President George Washington" and the date (Prucha 1971,
8–10, 76–77). In the portraits of Red Jacket painted in the
1820s, Red Jacket is always wearing the medal although the
inscription is altered to read "George Washington/Red Jacket/
1792," which reinforces the Red Jacket-Washington association but does not correspond to the design on the actual

medal now in the possession of the Buffalo and Erie County Historical Society.

In the fall of 1792, from September 30 to October 9, an Indian council was held at Au Glaze in Ohio. The Indians of the Ohio country were determined to resist American advance into their territory and wanted to know the attitude of the Six Nations. Red Jacket, named "Cowkiller" in the British transcripts of the council, advised the council to seek peace with the Americans. The principal speaker for the Western Confederacy at the council then accused the Six Nations of hiding their real purpose in coming to the council, implying that the Six Nations were not speaking for themselves but were acting as messengers for the Americans. Red Jacket, as the speaker for the Six Nations, replied that it was well known that they had been speaking with the Americans and proceeded to relay Washington's proposals to give compensation in exchange for land. Messquakenoe, speaking for the Western Confederacy, rejected the proposal and insisted that the Ohio River was the proper boundary. Red Jacket's final speech at the council promised that the Six Nations would "join with you and will put our heads together and endeavour to get all our lands back" (Simcoe 1923, 218–29). Red Jacket's expressions of unity stopped far short of a commitment to ally with the western nations in a military conflict with the Americans.

On November 13–14, 1792, after the delegation had returned from Au Glaze, the Six Nations, with British and American agents, held a council at Buffalo Creek. Red Jacket reviewed the events of the late council and invited representatives of both the British and United States governments to attend a council in Sandusky the following spring and asked the United States to appoint "sensible people" to attend and to bring with them "all Records of purchases of Lands, Treaties and Documents, Maps, &c., since the first arrival of the white people among us" so that they could be reviewed.

Later, Israel Chapin responded to Red Jacket's invitation on the part of the United States. Red Jacket repeated his wish that the delegates be "not only good persons, but sensible proper people no Land Jobbers but such as Colonel Pickering" (Simcoe 1923, 1:256–60; Bingham, 1931, 94-102; *ASPIA* 1:337).

Hopes of a resolution of the troubles in 1793 came to naught. In May three American Commissioners, Timothy Pickering, Benjamin Lincoln, and Beverly Randolph, prepared to make the trip. Traveling also was a delegation of Quakers from Philadelphia Yearly Meeting, who were to act as observers and ensure fair treatment. Quakers meshed with Pickering's aims of peace and gradual civilization of the Indians.

The Quakers encountered Red Jacket and others along the Genesee River, and Red Jacket made a humorous reference to the proposals of Pickering and the Quakers that the Senecas should turn from hunting to raising sheep and cattle. "[W]hen he [Red Jacket] was in Philadelphia, the white people had proposed a method for them to turn buffaloes [*sic*] into cows, deer into sheep, and bears into hogs; he thought it now a fit time for the commissions to show them a piece of their skill; as they were now on their way to Canandaigua . . . and a good buffaloe would be very agreeable for provisions along the way" (Moore 1835, 292).

On June 11 the commissioners met with the Indians in council at Buffalo Creek. All appeared in readiness. The Senecas were represented by two groups, one headed by Red Jacket and the other by Captain Billy. After several conversations with Governor Simcoe, the American party finally reached Detroit in mid-July, only to be left waiting while the Indians were in council at Sandusky. On August 11 the interpreter, Jasper Parrish, arrived in Detroit, bringing a speech by Red Jacket who had remained in New York. Red Jacket explained that Brant had opposed their coming. Red Jacket also explained that he feared that there would be war, and if the Six Nations came, they might be drawn into the conflict. He further advised Pickering to speak privately with the chiefs of the Six Nations to convince them not to join in the war. The contact should be kept private, however, so that the hostile Indians would not know that the Six Nations were acting under the influence of the United States (Pickering Papers, 59-204).

The American commissioners left Detroit in August 1793 without having met with the hostile tribes. Peace seemed remote. In October 1793, February 1794, and April 1794 the Six Nations met in council at Buffalo Creek with representatives of the British and American governments. The Americans were clearly worried that the Six Nations would join the Western Confederacy. The unease continued throughout the summer, with rumors reaching Fort Pitt that the Six Nations, at the insistence of the British, were coming to attack American forts and settlements. The issue was particularly critical in the Erie triangle, the parcel of land connecting Pennsylvania to Lake Erie. Pennsylvania wanted to begin settlement, but the Seneca continued to claim the territory (Campisi and Starna 1995, 477–78). In contrast to his very visible role in 1792 Red Jacket said little in the councils at Buffalo Creek in 1793 and 1794. Cornplanter, Joseph Brant, and Farmer's Brother were the speakers for the Six Nations.

The Treaty of Fort Stanwix in 1784 and the land concessions of the following years had been a source of bitterness to the Six Nations. Now, there was a new willingness on the part of the United States to reach a more amicable resolution to the problem. Timothy Pickering, the American commissioner at the Treaty of Canandaigua, said bluntly during the treaty negotiations that "he did not approve of the commissioners at fort Stanwix—that they had just then become conquerors, and the Indians must make some allowances if they spoke harshly and proudly to them" (Savery 1837, 356). Issues of war and peace in the Ohio country and the friction between the Six Nations over the ownership of Presqu'Isle and the Erie triangle made the situation dangerous. Confronting a hostile Indian Confederacy in the Ohio country, the United States was not disposed to have a potentially hostile Six Nations on their northern flank.

The war in the west formed a backdrop to the treaty. The decisive Battle of Fallen Timbers was fought on August 20, 1794, but accurate information about the outcome did not reach western New York until October. Local whites had been nervous all summer (Turner 1851, 305–7, 409, 411; Stone 1841, 128–29). Their fears were, in part, justified. Joseph Brant was preparing to bring warriors to the aid of the western Indians when word was received of Wayne's victory (Kelsay 1984, 510–15).

Pickering arrived at Canandaigua in September. Buffalo Creek was too close to the British, who would continue to garrison Fort Niagara until 1796, and Pickering wanted to separate the Six Nations from British influence. Although the treaty is written as between the Six Nations and the United States, the Mohawks were absent and the Tuscaroras were scarcely mentioned. Present also at the treaty was a delegation of Quakers from Philadelphia Yearly Meeting, who had been asked to ensure the fairness of the proceedings.

The Iroquois began to arrive in mid-October, and the negotiations lasted from October 14 to the signing of the treaty on November 11. Several speakers represented the Iroquois. Red Jacket first spoke on October 23 as the orator for the women (Savery 1837, 355–56). He was also present in the discussions between the Indians and the Quakers on the nature of the treaty.

The major issues involved land. The western boundary of the Six Nations established in the Fort Stanwix treaty was a line from the mouth of Buffalo Creek south to Pennsylvania. This line cut off not only the Ohio country but the disputed Erie triangle and villages in western New York.

Pickering was unwilling to discuss the Ohio lands and informed the assembled Indians that they, specifically Cornplanter, had received payment for the Pennsylvania lands. Pickering, however, was willing to concede the territory in New York State west of Buffalo Creek, a tract considerably larger than the lost Erie triangle.

In the discussion of the Erie triangle, Cornplanter had taken the major part. The discussion then turned to the remaining land issue, specifically to the four-mile wide strip along the Niagara River from Fort Schlosser south to Buffalo Creek, which had been taken at the Treaty of Fort Stanwix. Pickering wanted to retain the land, but Red Jacket feared white settlement and wanted to retain fishing rights in the Niagara River. In the end, Pickering, desiring to complete the treaty, conceded the land, reserving only the right to build a road to Buffalo Creek.

Red Jacket spoke several times in the treaty negotiations. He desired peace and a resolution to the problems between the United States and the Six Nations, but he also was wary of the desire of the United States for Indian lands:

> You white people have increased very fast on this island which was given to us Indians by the Great Spirit; we are now become a small people, and you are cutting off our lands piece after piece—you are a hard-hearted people, seeking your own advantages.

> I see there are many of your people here now, watching with their mouths open to take up this land [referring specifically to the four-mile strip]; if you are a friend to us, then disappoint them. (Savery 1837, 362, 363)

The final treaty, signed November 11, 1794, pledged peace and friendship between the United States and the Six Nations. It acknowledged the existing Oneida, Onondaga, and Cayuga reservations. It defined the Seneca lands, bounded on the east by the line of the Phelps-Gorham Purchase and extending to the western border of New York. The United States had, at Canandaigua, returned land taken from the Six Nations one decade earlier. In return, the Six Nations renounced all claim to land outside of the defined borders and granted the right of the road to Buffalo Creek. The United States also presented the Six Nations with ten thousand dollars in goods, and increased the annual annuity by three thousand dollars. Ten years after Fort Stanwix, the Six Nations had a legitimate treaty. Peace had finally come to the Iroquois in New York State.

The treaty is worded as being between the United States and the Six Nations, but it might be better described as a treaty between the United States and the portion of the Iroquois Confederacy remaining in New York. The Mohawks and other Iroquois living in Upper Canada were not parties to the treaty. Absent also from any consideration at this time were the Mohawks living at St. Regis in New York and across the border in Lower Canada (Quebec). The major land issues resolved by the treaty—the Erie triangle, the western boundary, the four mile strip along the Niagara River—were all matters principally concerning the Seneca.

The treaty had a complex history, and many people spoke for the Iroquois during the negotiations between 1790 and 1794 that led up it. The treaty is sometimes referred to as the "Pickering Treaty" in recognition of his role as the agent of the United States. The Iroquois did not assign such responsibility to a single individual. Red Jacket spoke frequently, but spoke usually to express the collective views and decisions of the Indians. But there is reason to think of the Canandaigua treaty as the joint product of Pickering and Red Jacket. The successful conclusion of the treaty was the result in large measure of Pickering's willingness to understand the Iroquois concerns and to respect the Iroquois manner of negotiation. His teacher in both areas had been

Red Jacket. Who benefited more from the treaty and the treaty's effect on the status of the Senecas is a matter for debate (Campisi 1988, 60–65).

5

The Sale of the Seneca Lands,
1795–1802

In 1795 the Connecticut Land Company gained title to a portion of the Western Reserve lands in northeast Ohio. Joseph Brant, despite the provisions of the Canandaigua treaty of 1794, claimed the land for the Six Nations in Canada. Although it was a weak claim, the Connecticut owners were willing to negotiate, and they met with Brant, Red Jacket, and others of the Six Nations at a council at Buffalo Creek in June 1796, agreeing on a settlement of fifteen hundred dollars to extinguish the Indian claim (Kelsay 1984, 542–43). Red Jacket is reported to have made another nativist speech on this occasion: "You white people make a great parade about religion; you say you have a book of laws and rules which was given to you by the Great Spirit, but is it true? Was it written by his own hand and given to you? No, it was written by your own people. They do it to deceive you. Their whole wishes center here (pointing to his pocket); all they want is the money" (Blanchard 1880, 227).

The following year, Red Jacket visited Hartford, Connecticut, and there lamented the condition of the Seneca: "We stand on a small island in the bosom of the great waters. We are encircled,—we are encompassed. The evil spirit rides upon the blast, and the waters are disturbed. They rise, they press upon us, and the waves once settled over us, we disappear forever. Who then lives to mourn us? None. What marks our extinction? Nothing. We are mingled with the common elements" (Stone 1841, 164).

The treaty between Great Britain and the United States in 1783 established the Great Lakes as the boundary between Canada and the United States. The British, however, continued to garrison Fort Niagara, on the United States side of the Niagara River and several forts in the west as well until 1796. When the control of Fort Niagara passed to the Americans, the new commander, Captain James Bruff, invited the Seneca chiefs to a council. At the council, held September 21–23, 1796, Captain Bruff presented the Senecas with an American flag and requested permission to widen the road from Avon to Fort Niagara. Bruff noted that Senecas had been employed by the British to capture deserters from the British garrison at Fort Niagara who were attempting to reach the American settlements east of the Genesee River. They could no longer do this, Bruff told them, because the boundary between the United States and British territory was the Niagara River (Turner 1850, 347–48; Benn 1996, 54–56).

Red Jacket was fully aware of the implications of the speech. In an unusually blunt reply, Red Jacket characterized the Americans as a "cunning people" not to be trusted. He expressed surprise that Bruff should say that the Senecas were within the boundaries of the United States. This was news to Red Jacket, who countered that their lands lay between those of the United States and Great Britain, and could not be considered as being within the boundaries of the United States.

Red Jacket then turned to a more immediate threat. The Senecas understood that Thomas Morris, the owner of the pre-emption right, was seeking to purchase their lands in western New York. The Indians were disturbed in their dreams, continued Red Jacket, by the vision of a "great eater with the big belly" who might prove to be too clever for the Indians. Since the Indians understood that no one could negotiate with them for the purchase of land without Congressional approval, Red Jacket appealed to Captain Bruff, as a representative of the United States government to tell Congress not to license Morris or allow him to purchase any Indian land (Talk of the Senecas . . . Sept. 23 [1796], in O'Reilly Collection).

After Red Jacket had spoken, Farmer's Brother spoke on behalf of the women, who owned the land. The women thought that widening the road was a good idea, but said that they too were disturbed in their dreams and requested that Morris not be allowed to purchase their lands.

The "eater with the big belly" was Robert Morris (1734–1806). Phelps and Gorham, who had owned the right to purchase the Seneca lands west of the preemption line, had purchased the lands east of the Genesee River and a twelve-mile-wide tract west of the Genesee River above Avon, New York, but, because of their financial condition, relinquished their preemption rights to the rest of the state to Massachusetts in March 1791. Massachusetts promptly resold the preemption right to Robert Morris. The tract was estimated to contain almost 3,800,000 acres. Morris also purchased, in 1790, the bulk of the Phelps-Gorham purchase of 1788 (Turner 1850, 396–97; Morris, Pioneer Settlements, 2–3, in O'Reilly Collection).

In 1791 and 1792 Robert Morris sold his western New York land rights. The vast majority of it was sold to a group of European investors organized as the Holland Land Company. That land acknowledged in the Treaty of Canandaigua as the property of the Seneca, but Morris had the sole right to purchase. Morris's land sales to the Holland Land Company and others were made on the condition that he would be able to extinguish the Seneca titles.

Until the Senecas agreed to a sale, the land remained their property. Robert Morris remained in Philadelphia. His son, Thomas Morris, ably looked after his land interests in western New York. The younger Morris had first visited the Seneca country in 1791, had moved to Canandaigua in 1792, and was well acquainted with the Seneca. Much of what is known about the events of the 1790s, particularly of the negotiations for the sale of the Seneca land at Big Tree in September 1797, derives from Thomas Morris. Morris recorded those proceedings in detail in records now included with the Thomas Morris material in the O'Reilly Collection at the New-York Historical Society. A similar "Diary of Proceedings" of the Big Tree negotiations, prepared by Thomas Morris or his associates, is included in the archives of the Holland Land Company, microfilmed by the State University of New York at Fredonia (File 137). Morris was a key informant for William L. Stone (1841) and Henry O'Reilly (1838). In 1844 he wrote a lengthy memoir of the "Pioneer Settlements in Western New York" about his experiences between 1790 and 1797, which is now part of the O'Reilly Collection at the New-York Historical Society.

The speech made by Red Jacket to Captain Bruff at Fort Niagara on September 23, 1796, had been sent on to President Washington. Because a treaty with the Six Nations required the consent of the governments of the United States and Massachusetts, it was first necessary to counteract the effect of that speech. In February 1797 Thomas Morris convinced Cornplanter and Joseph Brant to go to Philadelphia where Cornplanter expressed his willingness to see a part of the land (Wilkinson 1953, 262). President Washington appointed a commissioner on March 2, 1797, noting that the consent of the Indians was a prerequisite to holding a treaty (*ASPIA* 1:626). Morris then traveled to Buffalo, where he met with Red Jacket and Farmer's Brother, taking care not to let them know of the earlier approach to Cornplanter. At Buffalo Creek Thomas Morris took Red Jacket to task for his remarks of the past September, and Red Jacket said that his words had been spoken in jest. He was willing to hold a conference (Wilkinson 1953, 262–63). Over the next several months Thomas Morris worked to gain additional consent and succeeded in getting a statement from Red Jacket that he had spoken in jest when he called Robert Morris's father "the great Eater."

Red Jacket's retraction may have been in part through a reluctance to insult the father in the presence of the son or may indicate that Red Jacket, like the other Senecas, was being convinced by the promises of Thomas Morris (Wilkinson 1953, 263). By the summer it had been agreed to hold a treaty at Big Tree (Geneseo) in August.

At the Treaty of Big Tree Thomas Morris and Charles Williamson represented Robert Morris; William Shepherd was the commissioner from Massachusetts; and Jeremiah Wadsworth was the commissioner for the United States. Morris arrived on August 26, but the council did not officially begin until August 28 with speeches from Shepherd and Wadsworth and with Morris reading a communication from his father. Red Jacket responded the following day on behalf of the Seneca, asking for more candor from Morris.

On August 30 Thomas Morris made his proposal in a lengthy speech. The lands of the Seneca, he argued, were largely unproductive. The Seneca could sell most of the land, retaining reservations adequate to their needs. The money from the sale would be invested in the bank, and the interest from the investment would make the Senecas rich and happy. Never again would the Seneca be offered such generous terms. The Indians retired to consider the offer, but on September 1, Farmer's Brother came to Morris with the unwelcome news that a local person had been selling whisky and many were now drunk, including Red Jacket, and in no condition to do business.

The following day, the whisky sellers having been removed, business resumed. Farmer's Brother opened the proceedings, but Red Jacket was the speaker chosen to respond to Morris's offer, saying that the Seneca preferred land to money and that the Indians had been cheated in previous dealings with the whites. Morris rose to assure them that he would make a generous offer. That night, Morris met privately with the principal sachems, offering one hundred thousand dollars for the whole of their lands to be invested in bank stock, which would bring them at least six thousand dollars annually. The sachems told Morris to make his offer in public council.

On September 3 Red Jacket privately informed Morris that the speech he delivered the day before did not represent his feelings and encouraged Morris to continue in his efforts. That afternoon Red Jacket again spoke against the sale but also asked Morris to put his offer in writing. Morris agreed, repeating that the Seneca would never again have such an opportunity and attempted to graphically portray the extent of his offer by describing the number of barrels that would be needed to hold that sum and the number of horses that would be required to pull the wagons filled with the barrels.

The offer created divisions among the Indians. By Morris's account, the sachems were in charge of the negotiations. Although Red Jacket's own status as a sachem is doubtful, at least in this instance he seems to have been acting as the spokesman for the sachems. The council continued with the sachems taking on the business. On August 6 Red Jacket repeated his earlier assertion that land was the source of the nation's prestige but added that the Senecas would be willing to sell a single township at one dollar per acre. Morris, who was under pressure from the other members of his delegation to bring the negotiations to a close, quickly rejected the offer and told the Indians that if this was to be their offer and if nothing more could be expected, then they might as well "cover the council fire" and declare the negotiations at an end.

Red Jacket immediately sprang up and agreed to Morris's proposition to end the negotiations. The Senecas were free to sell or not sell, and whichever course they took could not disturb the friendship that existed between the Indians and the United States. The Senecas were unwilling to sell any land. As there was nothing left to discuss, Red Jacket shook hands with Morris and announced that he had covered up the council fire. (Morris, "Pioneer Settlements," 35, in O'Reilly Collection)

The council was seemingly at an end. There had been a noisy demonstration of support for Red Jacket's words and actions on September 6. On the following day, however, Farmer's Brother came to Morris to apologize for Red Jacket's harsh words. Morris reminded Farmer's Brother that because he (Morris) had lit the fire, Red Jacket had no right to cover it over. The council resumed with Farmer's Brother, Little Billy, and Cornplanter speaking for the Seneca and Morris taking his appeal to the warriors and to the women of the Seneca.

By September 10 Morris's purchase offer had been accepted, and the next several days were spent drawing the boundaries of the lands that were to be reserved for the Senecas. Red Jacket had not participated in the public business of the council since his attempt to end it on September 6, but he now reappeared to try to preserve as much land as possible at Buffalo. Morris attributed Red Jacket's activity to his vanity as a chief and described what he regarded as totally unrealistic demands for land at Buffalo and Cattaraugus as a conflict between Red Jacket and Cornplanter. Red Jacket, however, spoke of national pride and honor that would be lost if too much land were surrendered.

The question of a reasonable size for the reservations had not been addressed in Morris's initial proposal, and it made it clear that if the reservations were too large, he would have to lower the purchase price. In the end the total area of the reserved lands amounted to approximately 340 square miles. Buffalo Creek was by far the largest, almost twice the size of Tonawanda, and more than three times the size of Alleghany, the home of Cornplanter. If the size of the reservation was a measure of status, Red Jacket was clearly the winner.

Morris's reminiscences record that Red Jacket came to him the night before the signing of the treaty, saying that he would not sign the document in the council house but would come to Morris later privately and sign. It would not do, Red Jacket said, to have the treaty go to President Washington without his signature, as Washington might then think that Red Jacket had lost his rank and influence among the Seneca. He requested that the blank space for his signature be left near the top of the document. This was done, and Red Jacket signed.

In Morris's account and in William L. Stone's account that derives from Morris, Red Jacket acts with duplicity. He publicly speaks against the sale but privately encourages Morris to proceed. He publicly opposes the sale but privately arranges to sign the document to maintain his status with the American government. From Morris's evidence it seems clear that Red Jacket and the other Seneca leaders were in favor of a sale of at least a portion of their lands. Red Jacket's speeches against the sale are equivocal, and I think should be seen more as bargaining points or attempts to raise his status among the warriors than a sincere determination to oppose any sale of land. From Morris's own account, however, it is also clear that Red Jacket, when his offer of the sale of a single township was rejected out of hand, attempted to stop the sale. When the sale seemed inevitable, Red Jacket tried to retain as much land as possible.

The Seneca reserved ten parcels of land: six small reserves along the Genesee River, ranging from two to sixteen square miles in size, the larger reservations of Cattaraugus, Allegany, Tonawanda, and Buffalo Creek, and a small parcel on Canadaway Creek. In all, the reservations totaled about 340 square miles. Over the next few years, as Joseph Ellicott surveyed the land for the Holland Land Company, minor adjustments would be made. The mile-square Oil Spring Reservation on Cuba Lake, somehow omitted from the 1797 treaty, was set aside for the Seneca in 1801 by Joseph Ellicott, and the Holland Land Company marked out the Tuscarora Reservation in what is now Niagara County, New York (Bingham 1937, 50–55, 86–95).

The Buffalo Creek and Cattaraugus Reservations were not exclusively Seneca. In 1816 Erastus Granger prepared a census of Indians in New York State. At that time, 1,879 Seneca were in the New York reservations besides 216 Onondaga and 125 Cayuga at Buffalo Creek, and 65 Munsees at Cattaraugus (Snyder 1978, 30). Although the Seneca continued to occupy the heart of their old homeland in the Genesee Valley until 1826, the geographical center of the Seneca Nation had moved west.

On June 30, 1802, the Seneca sold Little Beard's town, a two-mile-square tract near Geneseo, New York, for $1,200. The 1797 boundaries included lands along Lake Erie from the mouth of Eighteen Mile Creek to Cattaraugus Creek, and extending up Cattaraugus Creek. Another parcel included the lower portion of Canadaway Creek, and the adjacent shoreline of Lake Erie toward, but not quite reaching, the boundaries of the Cattaraugus Reserve. The separate Cattaraugus and Canadaway parcels were exchanged for a consolidated reservation along the Cattaraugus Creek, giving most of the Lake Erie front to the Holland Land Company. On August 20, 1802, a mile-wide strip of land along the Niagara River from Buffalo Creek to the Steadman farm, across from the northern tip of Grand Island, was sold to

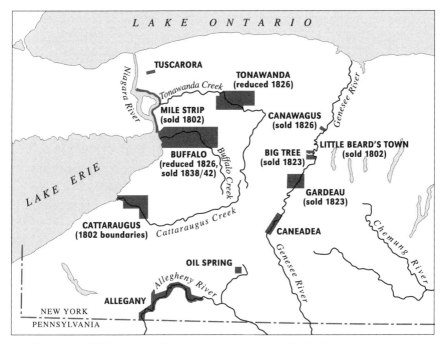

Seneca and Tuscarora Reservations in New York State, 1802–1826

New York State for $5,300 in money and $300 in goods. The 1802 sale did not include Grand Island or the other islands in the Niagara River. The Seneca retained the rights to fish, camp, and gather firewood along the river and were insured free passage across the Niagara River on the ferry at Black Rock (*ASPIA* 1:663–68; O'Reilly 1838, 118–19; Kappler 1904, 2:60–62).

In 1799 Handsome Lake had visions that became the basis of The "Good Message"—an important part of the Long House Religion as practiced on most of the Iroquois reservations to this day. The Good Message spread through the Seneca villages and later spread though the Iroquois world. The message included a continuation of the traditional ceremonies and teachings, some of which directly addressed the issues of cultural change and accommodation of the whites. There was a rejection of some aspects of the white man's culture, specifically alcohol, but also the recommendation that the Indians learn from the whites and adopt new ways of farming and appropriate technology (Wallace 1972, 280–82). In this respect the teaching supported, in part, the plans for instructing the Indians advocated by Timothy Pickering and George Washington in 1792 and the effort of the Quakers to teach new methods of farming and domestic economy at the Allegany Reservation beginning in 1798.

At a council at Geneseo on November 12, 1801, Red Jacket told Israel Chapin that the Indians were now willing to accept the proposals made by the president to learn the ways of the white people, to work the land with oxen, to make butter and cheese, to raise wheat, to learn to spin and knit. With the coming of the white people, the deer had fled, and the Indians now had to learn to make use of swine instead of bears and sheep in place of deer. He also stated that the Senecas were now willing to sell the mile strip of land along the Niagara River (Minutes of a council, Nov. 12, 1801, in O'Reilly Collection).

Handsome Lake and his half-brother Cornplanter traveled to Washington where Handsome Lake addressed President Thomas Jefferson on March 13, 1802, informing him that the Great Spirit had appointed him (Handsome Lake) to direct his people and that now Charles O'Bail (Cornplanter's son and Handsome Lake's nephew) and another Allegany chief named Strong were to speak for the Six Nations. His brother Cornplanter, Handsome Lake continued, was opposed by the sachems at Buffalo Creek, but the sachems at Buffalo Creek were all drunken men. The Indians had only a little land left, and they intended to hold it fast (US/SW/IA/LS A:183–87; Wallace 1972, 266–68).

Both Red Jacket and Handsome Lake were willing, in 1801 and 1802, to learn new methods of farming from the whites, but Red Jacket was not willing to accept the lead-

ership of Handsome Lake. Red Jacket let it be known that
he considered Handsome Lake the political tool of Cornplanter. Red Jacket observed to the Indian agent that when
"the Prophet" made speeches, his nephews sat on each side
of him, but when Red Jacket made sure others were sitting
next to Handsome Lake, the Prophet had nothing to say
(*Panoplist* 1807, 386–87; Wallace 1972, 290–91).

New York Governor DeWitt Clinton, who also believed
Handsome Lake to be the tool of Cornplanter, is the source
of the story of Red Jacket's trial. According to Clinton, in a
speech made to the New-York Historical Society in 1811,
Red Jacket was publicly denounced by Handsome Lake or his
followers at a council at Buffalo Creek as a witch. The crime
of witchcraft was punishable by death, but Red Jacket spoke
in his own defense for three hours, and his life was preserved
by a slim majority (Campbell 1849, 241–43; Wallace 1972,
259–60). Red Jacket's trial is the subject of a large painting by
Buffalo born artist James M. Stanley, which now hangs in the
Buffalo and Erie County Historical Society (Parker 1919, 325).

DeWitt Clinton appears to be the sole source for the
story of Red Jacket's trial, but there is other evidence of
open animosity between Red Jacket and Handsome Lake.
The *Port Folio*, a Philadelphia magazine, published an account of a council held on the Genesee River in June 1802.
In this story, published in 1811, the "Prophet of Alleghany"
counters a missionary with a strong denunciation of Christianity and the white men:

> They have driven your fathers from their ancient inherit-
> ance—they have destroyed them with the sword and poi-
> sonous liquors—they have dug up their bones, and left them
> to bleach in the wind—and now they aim at completing
> your wrongs, and insuring your destruction by cheating you
> into the belief of that divinity, whose very precepts they
> plead in justification of all the miseries they have heaped on
> your race. (*Port Folio*, 1811, 62)

In this account, Red Jacket is described as supporting the missionary in "pleading the cause of religion and humanity," and the council is reported to have decided that the Christian God was superior to the Great Spirit. It seems unlikely that Red Jacket was ever such a vigorous champion of Christianity. If this account is not entirely fictitious, it may be that the observer misunderstood the dynamics of a council where speakers would frequently restate the views of both sides to ensure that all properly understood the arguments.

On July 6, 1802, Israel Chapin wrote to the War Department about the prospects of the Seneca selling the mile strip on the Niagara River. Chapin reported that the Great Spirit had appeared to Handsome Lake and ordered that no more land should be sold, and Cornplanter declared that the president had told them the previous spring that the Indians must keep their land. Chapin wrote that the Indians had become strongly enthusiastic about Handsome Lake and those who were not were keeping silent (Chapin, in O'Reilly Collection). Red Jacket, however, had said that the Indians were willing to sell the mile strip in November 1801, and he participated in its sale in August 1802.

In Arthur C. Parker's translation of the "Good Message" of Handsome Lake, based on a version of the code written down by Edward Cornplanter (So-son-do-wa) in the early 1900s, Handsome Lake had a vision of Red Jacket carrying earth in a wheelbarrow. The heavenly messengers informed Handsome Lake that Red Jacket "was the one who first gave his consent to the sale of Indian reservations. It is said that there is hardship for those who part with their lands for money or trade. So now you see the doom of those who repent not. Their eternity will be one of punishment" (Parker 1913, 68; Wallace 1972, 259–60, 334–36, 368). Lewis Henry Morgan provides a variant, based on a translation by Ely Parker of the code as given by Sosehawa (Jemmy Johnson) at Tonawanda in 1848. In Parker's version, however, it is

Farmer's Brother and not Red Jacket who is being punished. In this version, Farmer's Brother moves a "heap of sand, grain by gain, and although he labored continually, yet the head of sand was not diminished" (Morgan 1851, 230, 254–55; Parker 1913, 11–12).

6

Defense of Seneca Traditions, 1802–1811

After the Treaty of Big Tree in 1797, the Holland Land Company began to survey western New York. Even before the company began to sell land in 1801, New Amsterdam—soon to be renamed Buffalo—had several houses and a tavern. The Senecas and other Indians at Buffalo Creek, Red Jacket's home, were no longer safely distant from the white settlements. Before, the Senecas had negotiated with the state and federal governments. Now they had to contend with white settlers as near neighbors.

Conflict arose between the Senecas and the other Indians living at Buffalo Creek and their new white neighbors. In May 1802 American authorities at Buffalo seized the goods of a Mrs. Thompson from Canada who came to trade with the Seneca at Buffalo Creek. Red Jacket, Farmer's Brother, and Young King broke into the storehouse where Mrs. Thompson's goods were stored and returned them to her. The Indian agent, Israel Chapin, was instructed by the secretary of war to impress on the Seneca the impropriety of their conduct. The Seneca apologized and said that they did not know the white man's laws (H. Dearborn to I. Chapin, June 15, 1802; I. Chapin to H. Dearborn, July 6, 1802, O'Reilly Collection).

A more serious incident occurred on July 25 in Buffalo. A group of white men were drinking and made a comment that attracted the attention of a passing Seneca named Stiff-Armed George. George asked three times what had been said, the last time in English. Getting no reply, he "flew in a rage" and with his knife wounded one man and killed a man named John Hewitt. George was arrested and imprisoned (Chapin to Dearborn, Aug. 1, 1802, O'Reilly Collection; *Albany Centinel,* Aug. 20, 24, 1802). Local historian Orsamus Marshall later stated that Stiff-Armed George had formerly been employed by the British to track down deserters from Fort Niagara and had a reputation among the whites for violence. Marshall also stated that George later joined the western Indians and was killed in the fighting against the Americans (Turner 1851, 374–75).

Red Jacket was the spokesman for a delegation of Seneca who traveled to Albany in August 1802 to discuss the proposed sale of a strip of land along the Niagara River. The fate of Stiff-Armed George was very much on their minds. Red Jacket was also very aware of the underlying jurisdictional issue. In addresses to the New York governor on August 18 and 20, 1802, Red Jacket reviewed the relations between the Indians and the United States. White people had committed five murders of Indians. In each of these cases the Indians had received "satisfaction" from the United States government in the form of presents. The perpetrators, however, often went unpunished. In no case was the white murderer punished by death. Despite the "satisfaction" it was clear that Indians and whites were held to unequal standards. Now New York was claiming that an Indian should answer to state law. Red Jacket stated that he believed that the Indians were answerable only to the United States and that they knew of no treaty with the state that bound them to give satisfaction although they were perfectly willing to treat with the United States. At the very least, the prisoner should be allowed to be freed on bond because imprisonment was a worse fate than death (NYS Legislature. Petitions, 90–402).

William L. Stone provides another variation of Red Jacket's sentiments:

> Since this accident has taken place, we have been informed that by the laws of this state, if a murder is committed within it, the murder must be tried by the laws of the state and punished with death.
>
> BROTHERS: When were such laws explained to us? Did we ever make a treaty with the state of New-York, and agree to conform to its laws? No. We are independent of the state of New-York. It was the will of the Great Spirit to create us different in color; we have different laws, habits, and customs, from the white people. We shall never consent that the government of this state shall try our brother. We appeal to the government of the United States. (Stone 1841, 177)

Stiff-Armed George was tried and convicted of the crime on February 23, 1803, at Canandaigua. Red Jacket was present at the trial (Stone 1841, 178–79). In the newspapers and in Orsamus Marshall's account Stiff-Armed George is presented as the aggressor. Jurors in the case, however, apparently had a different view of the matter and petitioned the state for a pardon, noting that white inhabitants of Buffalo had been guilty of "wanton and unprovoked attacks" on the Senecas, and in this case "had not the said George been pursued & beaten before any wound was given by him" there would have been no murder (NYS Assembly, Petitions, 385–87). Secretary of War Henry Dearborn wrote to Governor Clinton on February 14, recommending that George be pardoned if convicted, basing his appeal largely on the history of crimes against the Indians that had gone unpunished. Clinton pardoned George. The Stiff-Armed George trial brought up the issue of the extension of New York State to the Senecas, an issue that would be revisited in 1822 in the Tommy-Jemmy trial.

Red Jacket's popular reputation as the defender of Native American land and cultural traditions rests largely on speeches made in 1805 and 1811, which were widely republished during his lifetime and continue to be included in anthologies of Native American literature. The most famous of these speeches was delivered in 1805 to the Reverend Jacob Cram.

Rev. Cram had visited western New York on behalf of the newly formed Massachusetts Missionary Society in 1800 and again in 1803. In his report on the 1803 trip Cram noted that Red Jacket opposed Handsome Lake and "still appears to feel the gospel important." The New York Missionary Society was also sending missionaries to the Iroquois. Rev. Elkanah Holmes was politely rebuffed by Red Jacket on behalf of the Senecas in 1800, but in 1803 his proposal to build a "house" for "public worship" and the education of Indian children at Buffalo Creek was approved by an Indian council, representing local Seneca, Onondaga, and Cayuga Indians. Yet another missionary, Lemuel Covell of the Shaftsbury Association, was present at the council. According to Covell, the "famous orator, Red Jacket was a strenuous advocate for receiving the gospel and building a house, and the majority were on his side."

Covell's account of his missionary travels of 1803, published at Troy, New York, in 1804, contains the text of Red Jacket's speech on behalf of the council to Holmes and Holmes's extemporaneous reply. Covell is quite careful to document the occasion. The speech is followed by a testimonial to its accuracy. The interpreters are named, and their translation of the speech is witnessed by two other whites, a justice of the peace and an army officer. Red Jacket's speech itself ends with a request that a copy be sent to the New York Missionary Society and another retained by the Indians "so that if it should be forgotten by our old men, it may be seen and understood by our children hereafter." Other Indian speeches appearing in missionary publications, including Red Jacket's speech to Holmes in 1800, have similar validations.

Jacob Cram did not return to western New York until 1805. His journal of that trip, published in the *Massachusetts Missionary Magazine,* is a detailed account of preaching the gospel and his encounters with Christian and pagan Indians and the Quakers at the Allegany reservation. He revisited Buffalo Creek in November 1805 where he had what he termed "an interview with a number of the Chiefs and others of the Buffaloe Indians." Cram did not record a major speech by Red Jacket. His report of the encounter is brief: "I had learnt something of their objections to receiving missionaries, and wished to know if they were disposed to go into a discussion of the subject. Instead of complying with my request, they embraced the opportunity of stating their usual objections, and seemed not disposed to go into any [useful] inquiry" (*Massachusetts Missionary Magazine,* Apr. 1806, 3:436).

Cram then left western New York, apparently never to return. He continued his missionary activities on behalf of the Massachusetts Association but has now faded into historical obscurity—except for the link between his name and that of Red Jacket.

That was Cram's version. No further mention of the encounter between Red Jacket and Rev. Cram was reported until 1809 when an unnamed "gentleman" from Canandaigua sent copies of the Red Jacket speech and a 1798 speech by Farmer's Brother to the *Monthly Anthology* of Boston. The "gentleman" praises both speeches as great oratory: "The speech of Red Jacket, I think, discovers the same beauties of imagery, united with a shrewdness of remark, and an extent of information, far beyond what we should have expected to find in the wandering tribes of Indians" (Mar. 1809, 6:158).

The speech has been reprinted many times, and numerous minor variations and additions appear in the text (Robie 1986; Densmore 1987). The first known edition, from which all other later printings appear to derive, was published in the *Monthly Anthology and Boston Review* in April 1809 (6:221–24). The full text of the speech is given in the appendix.

The missionary begins by claiming that there is only one way to worship the Great Spirit and that the Indians had been living in "great errors and darkness." He then offered the aid of the Massachusetts Missionary Society (called the Boston Missionary Society in the text) to teach the Indians and asked if there were any objections.

Red Jacket responded on behalf of the Indians, expressing his pleasure that they could speak their minds freely and telling Cram that the Indians had agreed on their response. Before answering Cram, Red Jacket reviewed the history of the coming of the white man to "this great island" that the Great Spirit had made for the Indians. The Great Spirit provided animals for food and made the earth produce corn for bread. If the Indians had disputes about their hunting grounds, they were settled without the shedding of much blood. Then the white man came, saying that they were fleeing persecution and asking for a "small seat." The Indians gave the white men corn and meat, and in return the white men gave the Indians poison (liquor). Soon, whites wanted the Indians' land, and there were wars. Now, Red Jacket said, "we have scarcely a place left to spread our blankets. You are not satisfied; you want to force your religion among us."

Red Jacket then turned to the subject of religion. He noted that the white man's religion was written in a book, but if the Great Spirit had intended those writings for the Indian, why had he not already given them the book and the means to understand it? Why, if the answers were in the book, did white men disagree about religion? The Indians had a religion from their forefathers, which told them to be thankful, love each other, and be united. "We never quarrel about religion."

The Great Spirit made both the Indian and the white but, said Red Jacket, had given each different complexions and different customs, and the Indians were satisfied. But, he continued, they would wait to see the effect of Cram's preaching on whites in the neighborhood. "If we find it does them good, makes them honest, and less disposed to cheat Indians; we will then consider again of what you have said." Having finished, the Indians approached Cram and offered to shake hands. Cram refused, stating that "there was no fellowship between the religion of God and the works of the devil."

William L. Stone suggests that the tone of Red Jacket's response was in part a response to a "want to tact" on the part of the missionary but partially absolves Cram by stating that this was his first, or at least an early, address to the Indians (1841, 194–95). This portrayal of Cram as young or inexperienced is not correct. Jacob Cram (1762–1833), was a graduate of Dartmouth College (1782) and was an experienced missionary (Emerson 1911, 191; Cram, 1909; *Boston Recorder,* Jan. 11, 1834).

A later and shorter rebuff to a missionary was recorded by William J. Snelling and is sometimes included with versions of the Cram speech (Thatcher 1840, 294–95; Drake 1880, 596). Red Jacket responds to a missionary's account of Jesus by observing: "[I]f you white men murdered the son of God, we Indians had nothing to do with the matter, and it is none of our affair. If he had come among us we would have treated him better. You must make amends for that crime yourself" (*New England Galaxy,* July 12, 1833).

On a superficial level Red Jacket's rejection of the missionary in 1805 seems to stand in contrast with his acceptance of a missionary station in 1803. Perhaps the change in attitude is a product of the influence of Handsome Lake. It is also likely that both Cram and Covell were far too optimistic about the implications of Red Jacket's earlier speeches. Although Red Jacket did indeed speak of the Indians "laying hold of the gospel" in 1803, it seems to me that in his mind the "gospel" was connected with white man's technology. What Red Jacket agreed to in 1803 was the offer of educational and technological assistance, promising only a fair hearing and the possibility that the younger people would adopt the new ways. Even while making these concessions, Red Jacket informed Holmes that the Indians continued to celebrate some of their traditional customs.

Unlike the documentation included in the pages of the *New York Missionary Magazine* for Red Jacket's speech of 1800 or in Covell's report of the 1803 speech, the documentation of the "Reply" is, at best, thin. It was sent by an unnamed "gentleman" from Canandaigua. The prefatory material mentions the presence of the U.S. Indian Agent and an interpreter at the speech, but names neither. William L. Stone, in his 1841 biography of Red Jacket, identifies his source for the encounter between Cram and Red Jacket only as a "distinguished gentleman, of high character and intelligence, then a resident of the Seneca country." The identity of this gentleman remains a mystery. The date for the speech is also a problem. The published versions of the speech date the encounter as the summer of 1805, whereas Cram did not reach Buffalo Creek until November.

Another piece of evidence is in the manuscript collections of the Buffalo and Erie County Historical Society. These papers include a manuscript copy, made in 1822, of a speech given by Red Jacket to Rev. Cram in 1805. This text identifies the whites present as Col. Chapin (Dr. Israel Chapin), Erastus Granger, and the Rev. Cram and purports to be Chapin's record of the speech. The text, however, varies considerably from the versions that have circulated in print. In this version Red Jacket focuses on the failure of attempts to educate Indians, who thereby lose the virtues of Indian society while taking on the vices of white society. Whites are avaricious; Indians have all that they need. Perhaps, Red Jacket considers, this is because the white men murdered the son of the Great Spirit. After contrasting the contentment and happiness of Indian society with the evils of white society, Red Jacket suggests that the white men relinquish their religion and follow that of the Indian.

What is the relationship between the version of the reply to Cram first published in the *Monthly Anthology* in 1809 and what one might call the Chapin version as preserved in an 1822 manuscript copy? Cram only mentions one encounter with Red Jacket in 1805. Perhaps Chapin's version is the authentic reply to Cram in 1805, and the version first published in 1809 was delivered on some other occasion. Possibly the material in the Chapin version was included in the original speech but omitted in the published version. Because Red Jacket's words on this and other occasions are known only through the filters of white translators and reporters, who may have had their own agendas to pursue, it is well to be cautious of words attributed to him. There is nothing in the printed versions of the Cram speech, however, that Red Jacket did not repeat on other occasions. The Chapin version also seems in keeping with the general sentiments of Red Jacket about the uselessness of white culture to the Indian although Red Jacket's suggestion that whites would be happier if they adopted the Indian's religion is not repeated in later speeches.

The speech proved quite popular. It, and the accompanying speech by Farmer's Brother, were reprinted in the *National Intelligencer* of Washington, D.C., in October 1809 and in James D. Bemis's *Ontario Repository* at Canandaigua later that same month. Bemis also published the two speeches in

1809 as a pamphlet titled *Indian Speeches*. The following year they were reprinted in the *American Register* of Philadelphia and anthologized in *Speeches Delivered by Several Indian Chiefs*. By 1816, after having appeared in magazines, newspapers, and pamphlets both in the United States and England, it is included, along with several other speeches by Logan, Red Jacket, and Farmer's Brother, in the *American Speaker*, a textbook of speeches intended for rising generations of American scholars. These speeches "abound in so many beauties . . . that an American youth cannot be too proud of those savage models."

The speeches are presented in the *American Speaker* and elsewhere as great oratory but without comment about how they were to be understood by their non-Indian audience. Why was an Indian speech denying the special revelation of Christianity so popular in the first quarter of the nineteenth century? The published texts commend the speech for its literary qualities, but it is very likely that there was more involved here than oratorical skill.

It was not the first time an Indian had questioned the special revelation of Christianity. A similar speech, delivered by an unnamed Indian to a Swedish missionary in 1710, had been reprinted several times in America and England in the eighteenth century and was included with the Red Jacket speech in the 1810 pamphlet of *Speeches Delivered by Several Indian Chiefs*. Both the 1710 speech and the Red Jacket speech of 1805 make similar claims for Indian religiosity and Indian morality and question the supposed moral virtues of the white man.

The portrayal of Indians as virtuous, religious, and moral beings may have particularly appealed to Samuel Wood, the New York Quaker publisher of the 1810 collection. Quakers felt that grace was universal, even where the special revelation of Christianity was unknown. To Quakers and others the Indian claim to be both moral and religious, even without knowledge or understanding of the Christian message, was a validation of their own religious beliefs. The image of Red Jacket confounding the Reverend Cram also appealed to those Americans who were skeptical of the claims and actions of the evangelical churches in general—and missionaries in particular. The first appearance of Red Jacket's "Reply" in a Boston publication, in the city that was also headquarters to the Massachusetts Missionary Society (tellingly misnamed the "Boston" Missionary Society) may be significant. Perhaps the editor was as interested in making fun of the claims of local missionaries as he was of informing his readers about Indian speeches.

Although one is left to speculate about the motives of the first publishers of Red Jacket's speeches in 1809 and 1810, there can be no doubt that at least some readers applauded Red Jacket's attacks on the pretensions of Christian missionaries. The approval of Red Jacket's sentiments is explicit in the pages of *Plain Truth* an anti-Calvinist and antimissionary magazine published at Canandaigua, New York, between 1822 and 1824. This publication reprinted both the "Swedish Missionary" speech and Red Jacket's "Reply" and more current material. Commenting on the "Swedish Missionary" speech, *Plain Truth* editorialized about the "dark and threatening aspect" of the "missionary fever" and hoped that the speech would furnish an antidote to it or

> induce some person to furnish us with some cogent or plausible reason why we should neglect the suffering poor at our doors, and contribute money for the propagation of the vices of civilization among a people, who, before the introduction of white men among them never took the name of God in vain—never knew such a crime as intemperance—and whose religion, more effectively than any Human Law, guarded them against every vice which disgraces the character of a Civilized People. (*Plain Truth,* Dec. 12, 1822)

The editor of *Plain Truth* had two points: first, that true religion is not dependent on being able to quote scripture or subscribe to a particular creed and second, that perhaps the Indians were closer to the "Christian" ideal than were the missionaries and their supporters. The words of Red Jacket and the unknown author of the "Swedish Missionary" speech were being used to express the disagreements that some white Americans had with the growing evangelical and missionary movements of the nineteenth century.

In 1810 a new threat to the Seneca tenure in New York emerged in the form of the Ogden Land Company. The Holland Land Company still held the preemption right to purchase the remaining Seneca lands in western New York if and when the Senecas and Tuscaroras chose to sell. In 1810 the Holland Land Company sold their rights to 197,835 acres of reservation land to a group of investors headed by David A. Ogden for $98,917.50—fifty cents per acre. The Ogden Land Company hoped to realize not less than $3.00 per acre on their investment (Ogden Land Company Record Book, NYS Library, 25–35). If the Indians could be convinced to move west and sell their land, the Ogden Company would reap a huge profit. The Ogden Land Company aggressively pursued the acquisition of Seneca land for the remainder of Red Jacket's life and beyond, and its claims continued to affect Seneca land tenure well into the twentieth century (Hauptman 1988, 102–5, 117–18; Upton 1980, 45–46, 66–70).

Red Jacket's opposition to land sales was not absolute. His role at the major sale of Seneca lands at Big Tree in 1797, according to the testimony of Thomas Morris, was ambiguous at best, with a strong public opposition and a private acceptance. In later years Red Jacket agreed without recorded opposition to the sale of the Genesee reservations and to the sale of Grand Island in the Niagara River. In this Red Jacket was, perhaps, bowing to what he considered inevitable. The Seneca would have difficulty holding on to the entire tract of western New York, and the loss of the smaller Genesee reservations, islands surrounded by a sea of incoming white settlers, may have even been desirable because it would concentrate the Senecas on the larger reservations where they would have a better opportunity to maintain their independence from white control and white influence. Red Jacket's policy after 1810 was resistance to all attempts by the Ogden Land Company to purchase the larger reservations of Tonawanda, Buffalo Creek, Cattaraugus, and Allegany and resistance to any attempt to convince the Senecas to move west.

The Ogden Land Company's first attempt to purchase land came in May 1811 when it sent a Mr. Richardson to Buffalo Creek to meet with the Senecas at a council at Buffalo Creek. Red Jacket was chosen to reply on behalf of the assembled sachems and chiefs. The response was a firm denial. They liked the lands they lived upon. If they to sell and move west, they would be foreigners and strangers, despised by red and white alike. Besides, wherever they moved the whites would soon follow to kill the game and trespass on the land.

Red Jacket professed not to understand the Ogden Land Company's claim to ownership of the preemption right. The Great Spirit had given the lands to the Indians, and any claims by others were false claims. Besides, the Indians expected to deal directly with the national government, and Richardson had brought no "writings" from the president and had, therefore, not come by a straight path. Being so often mistreated by the Americans and by the British, the Indians resolved that they must take care of themselves and place no trust in either side. The Ogden Land Company was disappointed, but it would try again many times to achieve its aims.

At the same council a missionary from the New York Missionary Society, Rev. John Alexander, also made a plea for the conversion of the Indians. Red Jacket was again chosen to speak for the Senecas. Alexander in 1811 fared no better than Rev. Cram in 1805. The Indians who adopted Christianity, said Red Jacket, had become divided, drunk liquor, and learned to cheat, in short, learned the vices but not the virtues of the white man. This time Red Jacket elaborated on the nature of religion. "We do not worship the Great Spirit as the white men do, but we believe the forms of worship are indifferent to the Great Spirit—it is the offering of a sincere heart that pleases him." Then, pointing to Erastus Granger, the Indian agent, Jasper Parrish, the interpreter, and Jacob Taylor, the representative of the Quakers, Red Jacket commended them for their council and instruction. He specifically commended the Quakers for teaching them how to use ploughs. As for religion, "They tell us we are accountable beings, but do not say we must change our religion. We are satisfied with what they do."

The speeches to Richardson and to Rev. Alexander in May 1811 were printed later that year at Canandaigua, New York, by J. D. Bemis in a pamphlet titled *Native Eloquence*. This sixteen-page compilation included the 1805 speech of Red Jacket to Cram and the 1798 speech of Farmer's Brother. No direct source was given other than the notation on the title page that the pamphlet was "published under the revision of the public interpreter," presumably Jasper Parrish. Like the 1805 speech, the two 1811 speeches were quickly reprinted and circulated throughout the United States. Red Jacket's reputation to the general public as an orator was secured.

Red Jacket's 1805 speech to the Reverend Cram and his 1811 address to the Reverend Alexander are only partly about the white man's religion. Both speeches were also about land. Part of Red Jacket's speech is a review of the coming of the white men and the initial aid given to white men by the Indians, white men who then proceeded to occupy all of the Indians' lands. Red Jacket's claim is for reciprocal morality: Indians once aided whites, now whites could at least respect the remaining Indian rights to their lands and to their customary actions. Here, Red Jacket is mirroring the position of Quakers and other people sympathetic to the Indians in the Early Republic. Or, the Quakers are mirroring Red Jacket's position. Again, the connection is not explicit although Samuel Wood, the publisher of the 1810 pamphlet, is also the publisher for New York Yearly Meeting of the Society of Friends (Quakers).

As previously stated, the early printings of Red Jacket's speech present it only as a specimen of Indian oratory. The explicit endorsement of Red Jacket's political position in the "reply" does not occur until the 1820s. In 1822 the "reply" and similar statements are reprinted in the *Philanthropist,* an abolitionist and reform periodical published in Mount Pleasant, Ohio, with specific calls for the government to protect the remaining Indian lands in the eastern United States. It continued to be used in this fashion throughout the decade.

Red Jacket's arguments that the Indians had a right to their own lands and deserved fair treatment from the whites were quoted in the debates over the forced removal of the Cherokee Indians from Georgia in the early 1830s. Participants in the public discourse could assume that their audiences would recognize the name of Red Jacket and were likely to be familiar with his major speeches asserting the rights of Indians to retain their lands and culture against the encroachment of white land companies, missionaries and governments. By the 1830s, Red Jacket's speeches had been printed in school text books, in pamphlets, anthologies, magazine articles and broadsides. His major speeches are still being reprinted.

Through the wide distribution of his speeches in response to Cram (1805), Alexander, and Richardson (both 1811), Red Jacket had entered the consciousness of the American public. Most of the readers of these speeches likely had little awareness of or concern for the specific politics of Seneca-white relations in western New York, but they understood, rightly or wrongly, that Red Jacket voiced the common complaints of all Native Americans.

7

War, Diplomacy, and Land,
1807–1819

The potential of conflict between the United States and Great Britain and the reality of conflict between the United States and the Indian nations had been the background for diplomacy between the Iroquois and the United States leading up to the Treaty of Canandaigua in 1794. With the Canandaigua treaty and the temporary cessation of open conflict between the United States and the Indian nations in the Ohio country and the withdrawal of the British from Fort Niagara and other posts on the American side of the international border in 1796, a decade of peace came to the Senecas in western New York.

But events on the oceans and in the Ohio country would trouble the peace of the Senecas. In the "Chesapeake Affair" on June 22, 1807, the commander of an American frigate refused to allow a British ship to search his vessel for deserters. The British commander opened fire, wounding and killing American sailors, and removed four suspected deserters by force. Relations between the United States and Great Britain deteriorated and brought open war in 1812.

If war came, the British authorities in Canada feared an invasion of their territory by the United States, and they began working to secure the friendship, or at least the neutrality, of the nations along the border (Horsman 1958; Allen 1975, 67–71; Allen 1992, 109–22). The United States feared that the British were instigating an Indian war, particularly after hearing that Tecumseh and his brother Tenskawantowa, the Shawnee Prophet, were again organizing a confederacy of the western tribes. In its efforts to counter the British and Tecumseh the United States sought to enlist the diplomatic aid of Red Jacket and the Senecas to maintain Indian neutrality in the event of the anticipated war.

The position of the Iroquois had changed considerably since the end of the Revolution. Many Iroquois moved to the Haldimand Grant along the Grand River in Upper Canada, and a smaller number of Mohawks moved to Tyendinaga on the Bay of Quinte on the north side of Lake Ontario. Other Iroquois lived on reservations on the border between New York and Lower Canada (Quebec). The Iroquois nations were now separated from each other in reservations and surrounded by whites. How could they survive the coming conflict with their political rights and lands intact? How could Grand River and New York Indians maintain good relations with the governments of Canada and the United States, respectively, without becoming enmeshed in affairs that were not their concern and without having to fight fellow Iroquois?

On August 25, 1807, Erastus Granger wrote to Secretary of War Henry Dearborn that a delegation of western Indians had visited Buffalo Creek to learn what part the Six Nations would play in case of war (Babcock 1927, 24–25). This western delegation may have included Tecumseh (Tucker 1956, 132–33, 344). The following year a delegation of New York Indians, including Handsome Lake, Cornplanter, and Red Jacket, traveled to the Wyandot village at Brownstown, on the Detroit River, where Red Jacket urged neutrality in case of war between the British and Americans (Babcock 1927, 25; Norton 1970, 285–86).

In February 1810 Red Jacket led a delegation to Washington on behalf of the Six Nations to "keep bright the chain of friendship" between the United States and the Six Nations. Red Jacket mentioned some grievances, specifically that cattle and horses had been stolen from the Indians and that they had received no compensation for their losses from the agent. The main topic of his address, however, was the threat of war. Red Jacket charged that British agents in Canada were not only trying to turn the Indians in the west against the United States "but they sent a war belt among our warriors, to poison their minds, and make them break faith with you." Not satisfied with simply rejecting the belt, they had called a council of the Six Nations and "resolved to let our voice be heard among our Western brethren, and destroy the effects of the poison scatted among them." Twice, said Red Jacket, they had sent delegations to the west, urging that if war came between the white people, they should sit still and take no part on either side. "So far as our voice has been heard, they agree to hearken to our council, and remain at peace with your nation." Red Jacket also mentioned that in these embassies, they had expended $620; "This fact is known to your agents" (US/SW/IA/LR 1:529–36; ASPIA 1:804; Snyder 1978, 40–43).

In response, the government promised to live up to its treaty obligations and thanked the Six Nations for its diplomatic efforts. As for the threat of war, the United States desired peace. If war did come, the Six Nations should "keep still in their seats." The United States could punish its enemies and protect its friends, without involving the Six Nations (W. Eustis to Red Jacket, Feb. 23, 1810, in US/SW/IA/LS 6:16–18).

The efforts of Red Jacket and others to influence the events in the west continued. In August and September 1810 a large council was held at Brownstown, near Detroit, attended by the Wyandot, Ottawa, Chippewa, Potawatomi,

Shawnee, Delaware, Munsee, and the Six Nations. Red Jacket
spoke on behalf of the Six Nations, or, more accurately, that
portion of the Six Nations remaining in New York State, for
not only were there many of the Six Nations, including
some Seneca, in Canada, but some Senecas had moved to
Ohio after the Revolution and were living in villages along
the Sandusky River (Tanner 1987, 89). In his speech Red
Jacket urged friendship for the Americans and acceptance of
the new ways of living (Parker 1919, 79–80).

Although the main import of Red Jacket's remarks was
accommodationist, Red Jacket's policy was driven by his
sense of political realism rather than by a desire to assimilate.
William Hull, the territorial governor of Michigan, related
how Red Jacket had used his tomahawk to illustrate the
situation of the Indians since the arrival of the white man.
The hilt represented the original extent of their territory,
and Red Jacket put his finger on the middle of the hilt to
show their present position. If the Indians continued to move
west, he demonstrated by dropping the end of the tomahawk, they would soon fall off. That would be the end of
them (William Hull to Erastus Granger, Sept. 30, 1810,
Granger Papers).

The Six Nations in New York had relinquished all property claims to the lands in the Erie triangle and westward
into Ohio (but not to the islands in the Niagara River) in
the Treaty of Canandaigua in 1794, but now, acting in part
on behalf of the United States, they were reasserting their
right not only to participate in the affairs of the tribes in the
west but also to resume a place of primacy in the delibera-
tions of the councils.

Despite the stated official position of the Senecas for peace
and neutrality and their reassurances of their intention to
ally with the United States many whites were unsure what
might happen if war broke out between the United States
and Great Britain. William Stone recorded the belief that a

number of Seneca warriors from New York did, in fact, go west to join Tecumseh and fought with him against the United States in the Battle of Tippecanoe in November 1811 (Stone 1841, 217, 212).

Although the military power of the Six Nations had diminished after the Revolution, they were still part of the military and political balance of power between the United States and Great Britain along the United States–Canadian border. If there was to be war, the United States did not want a hostile Six Nations in alliance with the British and the western Indians on its northern border.

The continuing policy of the United States was to keep the Six Nations away from the coming conflict. The War Department wrote to Erastus Granger on April 7, 1812, to urge vigilance as they had heard a report that one hundred and fifty or more warriors from the Six Nations were prepared to join the hostile Indians in the west (US/SW/IA/ LS C:125). At a council held at Buffalo on May 25, 1812, Red Jacket reviewed the circumstances of the Iroquois involvement in the Revolution and the efforts of the British to induce the Six Nations to cross over into Canada (Ketcham 1865, 2:422–23; Snyder 1978, 46–47).

Meanwhile, Iroquois from New York and Grand River were meeting to discuss their positions in the coming conflict. In May or early June 1812 Red Jacket sent a message to Grand River addressed particularly to the Wolf Clan, urging neutrality and reminding them of the British failure to keep its promises after the Revolution. Young King sent a similar message, backing Red Jacket's position (Johnston 1964, 193–94). In early June a delegation of New York Indians came to a council at Grand River to repeat their appeal for neutrality. Red Jacket does not appear to have been present at this council, and a man named Billy spoke for the New York delegation, expressing his mistrust of both the British and American governments and his desire for neutrality. The

Grand River response clearly identified the Americans as the enemy and the English as friends and the willingness of those living at Grand River to join the English if attacked. The Iroquois in New York were living under the power of their old enemies, but the Iroquois at Grand River would never consider the New York Indians as belonging to the Americans and wished them to be preserved in peace (Norton 1970, 289–92).

The United States declared war on June 18, 1812. On July 6 Gideon Granger held a council with the Six Nations at Buffalo, outlining the causes of the war and repeating the wishes of the president that the Indians not take part in the war. Because he had reports, however, that some of the young men were restless and could not be controlled by the chiefs, he proposed that they join the Americans and receive the same pay and provisions as the American soldiers. Two days later Red Jacket responded, using the occasion to recall the agreements reached between the United States and the Six Nations at the Treaty of Canandaigua. The Seneca desired that the chain of friendship between them and the United States would remain strong. As for the war, Red Jacket regretted that the white people were fighting and noted that the Six Nations were in an "unpleasant situation" of living partly in the United States and partly in Canada. He would endeavor to convince those Iroquois living at Grand River to remain neutral in the conflict between Britain and the United States. The speeches of Erastus Granger and Red Jacket in July were quickly reprinted in Buffalo, the first book (a pamphlet of thirty-one pages) printed at that place. The council and the publication of the speeches reassured the inhabitants of western New York that the Indians living among them would remain neutral (Severance 1896, 385–414).

Throughout the war, the policy of Red Jacket and the Seneca was to defend their own land. Their alliance with the

United States was in part based on a belief in its power. Reportedly, British emissaries offered the Seneca tracts of land in Canada to support their cause. Red Jacket replied, "Where you get so much land? You go to war with the United States they take all Canada from you. Will you give me land in England then?" (*Buffalo Commercial Advertiser,* Mar. 31, 1851).

At the council in Buffalo Red Jacket asked the Americans not to accept any services of any Indian unless the Great Council agreed on their participation. In July, however, the Senecas received word that the British and their Indian allies had taken possession of Grand Island, which was Seneca Land. At a council in Buffalo held July 24, 1812, Red Jacket addressed Granger:

> BROTHER: You have told us that we had nothing to do with the war between you and the British; but we find the war has come to our doors. Our property is taken possession of by the British and their Indian friends. It is necessary now for us to take up the business, defend our property, and drive the enemy from it. If we sit still upon our seats, and take no measures of redress, the British (according to the custom of you white people) will hold it by conquest—and should you conquer the Canadas, you will claim it upon the same principles, as conquered from the British. We, therefore, request permission to go with our warriors and drive off these bad people, and take possession of our lands. (*Otsego Republican Press,* Aug. 21, 1812; Babcock 1927, 27; see also Parker 1919, 82, who dates the council as Aug. 4)

The Senecas had established their position. They were allies of the United States but would only join the fighting to defend their lands on the United States side of the border.

The Iroquois at Grand River and Tyendinaga, although more positive toward the British side, were also reluctant to involve themselves in the Anglo-American conflict. Some did join British General Isaac Brock at Fort George soon after war was declared, but it was not until September 1812 that they joined in force. The arrival of Indians from Grand River at the Battle of Queenston Heights on October 13, 1812, helped repel the American invasion of Upper Canada. (Stanley 1950, 155–58; Stanley 1963, 220–23; Allen 1992, 136–40).

Until June 1813 the general policy of the United States was to secure the neutrality of the Six Nations. In April 1813 the War Department proposed that the Six Nations on the Niagara frontier move to the Allegany Reservation until the danger had passed. On May 2, 1813, Jasper Parrish wrote to General Morgan Lewis that the president had not given permission for the army to accept the services of the Indians (Ketcham 1865, 2:427–28; Snyder 1978, 58–60). Indian Agent Erastus Granger explained government policy at a council in Buffalo in May. On their part, the Six Nations intended to remain on their land as neutrals, but, if the British crossed the Niagara River, they were resolved to "take up the hatchet with our warriors in the defense of our common country" (LLHS 1971, 2:1, 263).

The Six Nations on both sides of the conflict fought in their own manner. They made effective scouts and the native equivalent of light infantry, but their commanders sometimes questioned their usefulness (Calloway 1987, 217–20); Allen 1992, 123–48; Benn 1991, 61–67). Along the Niagara River in 1812 and 1813 Indians with the British forces— including Iroquois from the Seven Nations in Quebec— made life difficult for the American defenders of Fort George, and on June 24, 1813, a largely Indian force scored a decisive victory over an American force at the Battle of Beaver Dam, seventeen miles from Fort George (Stanley 1963, 225–26). The United States began to rethink its opposition to enlisting the Indians of New York.

On July 11 a British force raided Black Rock, which was the crossing point on the Niagara River just north of Buffalo.

General Peter B. Porter, the American commander at Buffalo and Black Rock, hurriedly organized a force to drive
off the British and was joined by a force of about forty
Senecas led by Farmer's Brother and Young King. The skir-
mishing at Black Rock marked the first time that the Senecas from New York were actively involved in fighting during
the War of 1812. (LLHS 1971, pt. 2:2, 223–27; Stone 1841,
241) There is no mention of Red Jacket participating in this
action.

In June 1813 the policy of the United States changed.
The American commander Henry Dearborn, solicited Indian volunteers, although the change in policy caused some
confusion to both Erastus Granger and the Seneca (Ketcham
1865, 2:428; Snyder 1978, 64–65). In July General Peter B.
Porter urged that Indians be sent to Fort George (Porter
Papers, A234, A242).

Shortly after the action at Black Rock, the Seneca warriors were organized into a company with Farmer's Brother
as captain, Little Billy and Pollard as lieutenants, Red Jacket
as second lieutenant, and Blacksnake as ensign (Babcock
1927, 107). Red Jacket, the "cow killer" of the Revolutionary
War, held a rank that recognized his importance as a civil
leader of the Seneca but was clearly subordinate in wartime
to Farmer's Brother. Farmer's Brother, born circa 1725, had
led the Seneca warriors in the attack on the British troops
from Fort Niagara at Devil's Hole in 1763 and had fought
as an ally of the British during the American Revolution.
Farmer's Brother was also an orator. His 1798 speech grant-
ing a tract of land to Horatio Jones and Jasper Parrish was
frequently reprinted with those of Red Jacket (Stone 1841,
409–19). A Buffalo resident claimed years later that when
Farmer's Brother was asked if Red Jacket would accompany
the warriors, he replied, "Me take Red Jacket long as Squaw"
(*Buffalo Commercial Advertiser,* Mar. 31, 1851).

The Indian participation was further legitimized at a council held at Buffalo Creek on July 25. Farmer's Brother opened the council and directed each village to speak for itself. Red Jacket spoke for Buffalo Creek. Red Jacket told the agent that their participation in the war was not voluntary. They would have been content to follow the advice of the president at the beginning of the conflict to remain neutral. The Americans had maneuvered them into a war that they did not want (Snyder 1978, 65–67).

Another council was held in early August. Red Jacket stated that the Indians intended to remain on the American side of the Niagara River to defend their own village and friends. After harsh words on both sides General Porter and Agent Granger finally induced the Indians to join the American forces on the Canadian side of the Niagara River (Porter Papers, A251). The warriors from New York then crossed the Niagara River to assist the American forces at Fort George and were involved in skirmishes with the British forces and their Indian allies (LLHS 1971, 2:3, 30–31, 36, 71). For the next few months this force helped guard Fort George, the fortress opposite Fort Niagara at the outlet of the Niagara River into Lake Ontario. On October 21, 1813, Red Jacket made a speech outlining grievances concerning the pay of the Indian troops, but his remarks demonstrated his support for the alliance between the United States and the Indians. "Let us unite," he said, "and in one season more we will drive the Red Coats from this Island. They are foreigners. This country belongs to us and the United States" (Snyder 1978, 71–72).

On December 10, 1813, the American commander at Ft. George withdrew across the Niagara River. Before doing so he set fire to the buildings in Fort George and all the houses in the adjacent village of Newark. Newark, now called Niagara-on-the-Lake, had been the first capital of Upper Canada and was still one of the largest villages in the province. Its destruction, supposedly to deny the oncoming British forces refuge during the winter, angered the British and Canadian forces and unleashed yet more destruction.

The British forces crossed the Niagara River on the night of December 18, 1813, and captured Fort Niagara by the next morning. Over the next few weeks British forces, in retaliation for Newark, destroyed all the settlements on the American side of the Niagara River from the fort to the village of Buffalo. Tuscaroras and Senecas joined the refugees fleeing back to the Genesee River to escape the destruction.

In the spring of 1814 the British held Fort Niagara on the American side of the Niagara River and Fort George and Fort Erie on the Canadian side. Though the British had captured and burned Buffalo, they did not occupy it, and by April the American forces were planning an invasion of Canada. In April and May General Peter B. Porter, working with Red Jacket, Erastus Granger, and Jasper Parrish, raised a new force of five hundred warriors from the Six Nations who would serve under Porter's command (Babcock 1927, 147; LLHS 1971, 4:386–91). On July 3 the American army, including militia and 550–600 warriors under General Porter, crossed the Niagara River and easily took Fort Erie. On July 5 the American and British armies clashed at Chippawa. Captain Pollard was the overall leader of the Indian forces. Porter placed Red Jacket, "in whose intelligence I had great confidence" on the extreme left of the line. The Americans attacked and at first were successful but then were forced to retreat. More American forces came up under the command of Winfield Scott, and it was the British turn to retreat. The battle ended as an American victory (LLHS 1971, 4:358–65; Strong 1841, 256–70; Stanley 1963, 227–28).

At Chippawa, Iroquois from New York fought Iroquois from Canada. After the battle Red Jacket proposed to American General Brown to send an embassy to the Indians serving with the British forces to propose a mutual withdrawal. This embassy was successful, and the bulk of the Iroquois, both from New York and Canada, withdrew and played no further role in the war (LLHS 1971, 4:367–68; Stone 1841, 272–73; Stanley 1963, 339–30). Looking back on the events in later years, Porter appears to have approved of Red Jacket's diplomacy, although in 1814 he appears to have held a different attitude. In a letter to Farmer's Brother and the other chiefs on July 25, 1814, Porter urges them to continue with the army. Referring to Red Jacket, Cornplanter, and Blue Sky, Porter said that if they did not wish to act for themselves, they should not try to dissuade others. Their conduct would be reported to the president, who had the power to reward and punish (Snyder 1978, 77–80). Although a few members of the Six Nations continued with the American Army through the remainder of the campaign, the Battle of Chippawa would be the last time that the Seneca engaged in battle as a distinct military force.

Red Jacket's conduct during the war won the approval of both Peter B. Porter and his aide-de-camp, Major Donald Frasier. Frasier, in an 1821 letter to the *Buffalo Patriot,* responding to criticisms of Red Jacket's military record, described Red Jacket as leading his men bravely at Fort George and Chippawa and spoke of his gallantry in the field (Bryant 1879, 363; see also Stone 1841, 275). Nevertheless, stories of his personal cowardice followed him. During the negotiations for the Buffalo Creek treaty of 1838, a Seneca named Little Johnson told Henry A. S. Dearborn that he had been with Red Jacket during the War of 1812, and the warriors had been in battle five times, but that Red Jacket was absent during the fighting and had never been in danger (Dearborn 1904, 204).

The Senecas had participated in the War of 1812 to preserve their lands. They had lost land as a result of supporting the British during the American Revolution, and the failure of the western Indians to stop the Americans in 1794 and again in 1811 confirmed Red Jacket in his belief that the British were unable to support their allies. Faced with the possibility of invasion in 1812, there was little choice but to support the United States. The "right of conquest" had been used against them before, and they did not intend that it would be used against them again.

Red Jacket had hoped that the Indians would be able to maintain neutrality in the conflict between Britain and America, but circumstances worked against it. He accepted war when it came and served credibly with the American forces. This support did not stop Red Jacket from insisting on just treatment of the Six Nations. He was no war leader, either in a military or diplomatic sense. His triumph came not at the Battle of Chippawa but later when he helped negotiate the mutual withdrawal of the Iroquois warriors from both the American and British forces.

As a result of the sale of their lands at the Treaty of Big Tree in 1797, later sales of small tracts, and several adjustments to reservation boundaries, the Senecas in 1817 were reduced to five small reservations along the Genesee River and four larger reservations in western New York. An 1817 report measured the five Genesee reservations at 31,648 acres; Cattaraugus at 26,880 acres; Allegany at 30,469 acres; Tonawanda at 46,209 acres; and Buffalo, by far the largest, at 83,557 acres. The total of the Seneca lands, including 640 acres at Oil Spring, amounted to 343 square miles. The other reservations in New York—the Tuscarora, Oneida, Onondaga, Stockbridge and St. Regis combined—totaled 51,920 acres, about 81 square miles. The report estimated the average value of these lands at six dollars an acre, not including improvements (NYS Legislature, Assembly Report, no. 19, Mar. 4, 1819).

The Senecas had participated in the War of 1812 to protect their lands, but the major threat to their lands was neither British nor military; it was the Ogden Land Company, owners since 1810 of the preemption right to purchase the Seneca reservations. As described in an earlier chapter, the Ogden Land Company was rebuffed in its initial attempt in May 1811 to convince the Senecas to sell their lands and move to the west, but with the coming of peace to the region in 1815 the Ogden Land Company renewed its efforts to purchase the land.

A move to the west was a distinct possibility. Iroquois Mingos were living in the Ohio country in the early seventeenth century. Mohawks and considerable numbers from the other tribes of the Six Nations had moved from New York to Upper Canada after the American Revolution. Some Senecas had moved to the Sandusky River in Ohio in the 1780s. After the War of 1812, the major portion of the Oneida, along with the Brotherton and Stockbridge tribes, would move to Indiana and then to Wisconsin. Indians were constantly being pushed west. Why should not the Senecas move to a land where they could enjoy their own way of life without the bother of white neighbors and meddling missionaries? Before the War of 1812, some Indians to the west had proposed that the New York Indians join them there. There was sufficient interest in the proposal for a delegation from New York to travel west in 1816 to view the proposed new land. On December 26, 1816, Jacob Taylor, the Quaker agent near the Cattaraugus Reservation reported that the delegation had returned but that the western Indians had refused to grant them title and Red Jacket was saying that the Senecas must be content with the lands that they now owned (Society of Friends, PYM, Indian Committee).

The Ogden Land Company continued to work toward the purchase of the Seneca land. Jacob Taylor reported to the Quaker Indian Committee on June 29, 1816, that Horatio Jones and Jasper Parrish were in the employ of the Ogden Land Company, but a "considerable majority" of the Indians were opposed to any sale (Society of Friends, PYM, Indian Committee). In an address to the president and the secretary of war dated January 4, 1818, the Six Nations informed them that they had told the Ogden Land Company that they did not wish to part with their lands (*Cherry Valley Gazette,* Nov. 19, 1818). When New York Governor DeWitt Clinton, in his opening address to the New York State Legislature on January 27, 1818, voiced his approval of the New York Indians moving to western lands, providing the move was free and voluntary, and that the Indians be adequately compensated for their land, the Senecas responded with an address of their own, dated February 14, 1818, sending Governor Clinton a copy of their January 4th address to the president so that he could learn their minds (Lincoln 1909, 2:915–16, 941–43). Secretary of War John C. Calhoun wrote to Indian Agent Jasper Parrish (the same individual suspected of working for the Ogden Land Company) on May 14, 1818, to express the policy of the president:

> He desires the removal of the Six Nations not only because it would be in the interest of the United States, but because he believed it would add to the happiness of the Indians themselves. Experience proves, when surrounded by the whites, they always dwindle and become miserable. . . . The president, however, by no means wishes that force or threats should be used to cause their emigration. (US/SW/IA/LS D:165–66)

The following July, another council was held to convince the Senecas to sell Buffalo Creek and Tonawanda and to concentrate on Allegany and Cattaraugus. Red Jacket responded for the Seneca on July 9, 1819. The Indians had been placed where they were by the "God of Heaven" for purposes known best to Him. The white man had no right to interfere. They had been told that they owned large and

unproductive tracts of land, but they needed all the land they
retained for timber and to make new fields as the ones they
were working wore out. He also commented on the proposal that they move to the Allegany Reservation. They had
seen the Allegany Reservation, and if the president considered that to be a fine tract of land, he was "disordered in
mind" (Snyder 1978, 94).

The following day July 10, 1819, a disappointed T. L. Ogden
wrote to Jacob Taylor, agent of Philadelphia Yearly Meeting
at the Canandaigua Reservation, evidently hoping to gain
the sympathy of the Quakers for his efforts. He described
Red Jacket as insolent and offensive, so much so that after
his speech a delegation of chiefs led by Pollard—but not
including Red Jacket and Abeel (Cornplanter)—called on
the United States commissioner to apologize for the offensive language used by Red Jacket (PYM, Society of Friends,
Indian Committee). The Quakers, however, proved to be
allies of Red Jacket and those Senecas opposed to the sale
of the New York lands.

Among the many anecdotes told about Red Jacket is the
story of his meeting one day with Joseph Ellicott, the agent
of the Holland Land Company, in the Tonawanda swamp.
Both sat down to rest on the middle of a log. Presently, Red
Jacket said, "Move along, Jo." Ellicott did, and Red Jacket
moved with him. A few minutes later, he again said, "Move
along, Jo." Again Ellicott and Red Jacket moved to the end
of the log. Then again, "Move along, Jo." This time Ellicott
replied that he could not move any further without ending
up off the log in the mud (Johnson 1876, 168–69). That was
Red Jacket's point. The white man wanted the Indian to
move along and move along. Now, Red Jacket was telling
Ellicott, the Senecas would go no farther.

8

———

"Pagan" versus Christian, 1818–1827

Red Jacket's popular reputation was based largely on his speeches to the Reverend Jacob Cram (1805) and the Reverend John Alexander (1811), which were widely reprinted. When delivering these speeches, Red Jacket had spoken on behalf of the Senecas, or at least those of Buffalo Creek and Tonawanda. However united the Seneca of Buffalo Creek may have been in rejecting missionaries in 1805 and 1811, by 1818, if not before, they were seriously divided on the wisdom of allowing missionaries on their lands.

In 1819 the pro-missionary Seneca entered into a covenant with the New York Missionary Society, and Jabez Hyde, who had been the schoolteacher at Buffalo Creek, became the first missionary (Howland 1903, 125–61). That same year, the pro-missionary Seneca reproached Red Jacket for anti-missionary statements made during a council with government officials (Alden 1827, 91–93). This admonition signaled the division of the Seneca into recognizable Christian and the so-called Pagan Parties. Whereas the American public viewed Red Jacket as the leader and spokesman of the Seneca, the War Department and the missionaries viewed him as a factional leader.

In January 1821 Red Jacket sent a message to New York Governor Clinton about the many incursions of the whites onto Indian lands. He had several grievances: whites stealing timber, horses, and cattle and whites interfering with hunting and fishing. He reserved his greatest criticism, however, for missionaries, whom he charged with creating confusion and disorder (*NYS Assembly Journal,* 1821, 392–94; *Reformer,* 1821, 141–43). Legislative relief was swift. An "Act Respecting Intrusions on Indian Lands" was passed by the State Legislature on March 31, forbidding any non-Indian from "settling or residing on Indian land" (NYS *Revised Statutes,* 1829, 3:375–77). The law was not immediately enforced against the missionaries, so in the summer of 1822 Red Jacket appealed to local Quakers to "use their influence to free them from Missionaries" now within their borders (*Christian Philanthropist,* 1822, 76).

New York Governor DeWitt Clinton shared Red Jacket's estimation of the uselessness of missionaries. Clinton, writing in 1810 about the Oneida, described the efforts of the missionaries of being "but little use," whereas the programs of technical assistance in agriculture and the mechanical arts offered by the Quakers to be "the only competent ones that can be adopted" (Campbell 1849, 188–89). Red Jacket and others in the Pagan Party seem to have been of two minds about the usefulness even of the educational programs of Quakers. The Quaker teacher at Tunesassa, near the Allegany Reservation, wrote in December 1820 of a report that Red Jacket and an Onondaga were to send off to Washington to "break up the [Quaker] school at Allegany" (Barton 1990, 17–18).

The Indian Committee of the New York Assembly, in rejecting a proposed modification of the 1821 act during the session of 1824, stated that the efforts of the missionaries made the conditions of the Indians worse rather than better (*NYS Assembly Journal,* 1824, 695).

Some whites also shared Red Jacket's mistrust of the
motivations of the missionaries. A Long Island Quaker visiting
Cattaraugus in November 1824 warned the Seneca about
"hireling priests" who caused divisions among white Christians (Townsend Hawhurst to Catteragus [*sic*] Indians, July
11, 1824, in Maris B. Pierce Papers). For their part, missionaries charged that Red Jacket was the tool of scheming
whites. The pro-missionary *Western Recorder* in March 1824,
contended that "white pagans" were behind Red Jacket and
would "drive everything but universalism and crime from
society if they could." The Universalist *Gospel Advocate,* published at Buffalo, took these remarks as a challenge. They
defended Red Jacket's actions and published allegations of
mismanagement at the Buffalo Creek mission (*Western Recorder,* 1824, 22, 24, 31; *Gospel Advocate,* 1824, 83–84, 94–96,
102–4). The Universalists, however, denied responsibility for
Red Jacket's actions.

The Reverend John C. Breckenridge, who spoke with
Red Jacket in Buffalo in 1821, offered a more elaborate
explanation of the forces behind Red Jacket. Breckenridge
felt that Red Jacket was ignorant of Christianity and "had
unfortunately been led by designing and corrupt men, who
were interested in the result" (Hubbard 1886, 299–300). These
designing men included not only the enemies of missions
but, evidently, land speculators who wanted to remove missionaries who, according to Breckenridge, served to protect
Indian lands and interests.

There was a factual basis to the fear of Red Jacket and the
Quaker from Long Island that missionaries would "eat the
land" of the Seneca. In the early 1820s the Episcopal missionary to the Oneida, Eleazar Williams (ca. 1789–1858) was
promoting the move of a major portion of the Oneida,
Brotherton, and Stockbridge Indians from their New York
lands to Wisconsin. Even the *American Missionary Register* in

1822 blamed Williams for giving the Indians cause to mistrust missionaries (*American Missionary Register*, 1822, 51).

In March 1824 Red Jacket and the Pagan Party succeeded in getting a court order to eject the missionaries from Buffalo Creek (Harris 1903, 342–45, 348–49; *American Missionary Register*, 1823, 373–75). The Christian Party of the Senecas and pro-missionary forces, however, were also active. They had petitioned the legislature in 1822, 1823, and 1824 to revise the act and permit non-Indian schoolteachers and missionaries to reside on the reservations. The law was amended on April 20, 1825, to permit "any schoolmaster, teacher or family of teachers" (missionaries were not named specifically) to reside on a reservation if invited by a majority or a "major part" of the Indians (NYS *Revised Statutes*, 1829, 3:377–78). By fall 1825 the Seneca mission was back in operation.

In May 1821 a Seneca woman named Kau-qua-tau was found dead with her throat cut near Buffalo Creek. A Seneca chief, Soonongize, also known as Tommy-Jemmy, was arrested and charged with the murder (*Geneva Palladium*, May 21, July 21, 1821; Letchworth 1874, 193–94). Tommy-Jemmy was arrested. Orlando Allen recalled that the morning after the arrest a group of armed and angry warriors gathered in Buffalo where Red Jacket "addressed them in a fervid speech, attacking the whites with fierce invective, and lashing the Indians into fury with his artful and fiery eloquence." Allen feared violence, but Captain Pollard stepped in and advised the warriors to return to their homes and "remain quiescent until an appeal to the white man's law and sense of justice should prove ineffectual" (Bryant 1879, 335).

Like many events in Red Jacket's career, there is a second version of the story. James Aigin, who knew Tommy-Jemmy and Red Jacket, also witnessed the events. In Aigin's account a warrant was issued for Tommy-Jemmy's arrest, but the constable was afraid to serve it. Pascal Pratt, who was friendly with the Seneca and spoke their language, agreed to serve the warrant. Pratt found Tommy-Jemmy at Red Jacket's house and explained the matter, and Red Jacket asked what time they should appear. The next morning, at the agreed upon time, Tommy-Jemmy, Red Jacket, and a large body of Indian men and women came to Buffalo. The prosecuting attorney asked Tommy-Jemmy if he were guilty. Tommy-Jemmy said that the council of his nation had condemned the woman and that he had carried out the sentence. If it was now necessary that he should die, he was willing to make the sacrifice for the good of his people. Aigin, unlike Allen, makes no mention of a threat of violence (Aigin n.d.)

Tommy-Jemmy was brought to trial in Buffalo in July. He did not dispute the facts of the case. The woman had been accused of witchcraft, was formally condemned by the assembly of chiefs, and Tommy-Jemmy had carried out the sentence. At the trial both Red Jacket and Captain Pollard testified about Seneca usages, and Red Jacket in particular took offense at the idea that the belief in witchcraft was absurd. He reminded the court that white men in Salem had executed witches: "What have your brothers [the Senecas] done more than the rulers of your people have done? And what crime has this man committed by executing in a summary way, the laws of his country and the injunctions of his God?" Red Jacket was then asked whether he believed in a Supreme Being and in future rewards and punishments, to which he replied: "Yes! much more than the white men, if we are to judge by their actions" (*Albany Argus,* July 27, 1821; also *Niles Weekly Register,* Aug. 4, 1821, 358–59).

During the trial Tommy-Jemmy was represented by John C. Spencer, who argued that the Senecas were an independent nation and because the alleged crime was committed on Seneca land, Tommy-Jemmy was answerable only to the Seneca, not to New York State. Red Jacket participated in the jury selection and the defense, in one case objecting to a potential juror who wore glasses (Aigin n.d.). The key issue became the jurisdiction of the New York courts, the same issue that was involved in the Stiff-Armed George case almost twenty years earlier. The jury in Buffalo ruled that the Seneca were an independent people and that the court had no jurisdiction over the case. The Buffalo court, however, referred the case to the Supreme Court of New York, which took up the question of Seneca sovereignty (*Albany Argus,* Aug. 17, 1821), but were unable to render a judgment. They referred the case to New York Governor DeWitt Clinton, who proposed a legislative remedy (*NYS Assembly Journal,* 1822, 594–96, 1000–1001, 1004).

The result was a law passed on April 22, 1822, which asserted that New York had the "sole and exclusive jurisdiction" of punishing crimes. But the legislature also acknowledged that Tommy-Jemmy's act had been done "under the pretence of authority derived from the councils of the chiefs, sachems, and warriors" of the Seneca, and under these circumstances it seemed expedient to grant him a pardon (NYS *Laws,* 1822, 202).

The white man's laws did not impress Red Jacket. In 1819 Red Jacket participated in the trial of an Indian at Batavia for the crime of breaking and entering the house of Joseph Ellicott and stealing some spoons. At the end of the trial Red Jacket made a speech, arguing that the Indians were allies, not subjects, of the whites, and the culprit ought to be delivered up to them for punishment. The court sentenced the culprit to life imprisonment, which Red Jacket considered excessive and unfair.

After leaving the court, Red Jacket passed a printing office, which displayed the arms of New York State, including figures representing Liberty and Justice. Red Jacket pointed to the statue of Liberty, and asked what it meant. "Liberty," he was told. He pointed to Justice, and asked what that statue meant.

Red Jacket. Portrait from William L. Stone,
Life and Times of Red-Jacket (1841),
based on portrait by Robert W. Weir.

"Justice," he was told. Receiving his answer, he asked another
question, "Where him live now?" (Stone 1841, 366–67).

In September 1820 John Lee Mathies painted Red Jacket's
portrait at Canandaigua (see *frontispiece*). Between 1822 and
1828, Red Jacket was sketched or painted by Henry Inman,
George Catlin (three times), Charles Bird King (twice), and
by Robert Weir. In all of his portraits Red Jacket wore the

Pencil drawing of Red Jacket by Henry Inman, 1823.
Courtesy of the Albany Institute of History and Art.
Bequest of Sarah Walsh DeWitt.

medal presented to him by George Washington. The medal becomes transformed from the "Washington Medal" into the "Red Jacket Medal," even though there were a number of others of the same design and provenance (Costa Nunes 1980, 4–20; Guennsey 1866, 323–26).

When George Catlin painted a full-length portrait of Red Jacket, probably in 1826, Catlin indulged Red Jacket in the wish that he had expressed, "that he might be seen standing on Table Rock, at the Falls of the Niagara; about which place he thought his spirit would linger after he was dead" (Catlin 1841, 2:104). Red Jacket's portrait by Robert Weir, painted in 1828, also features Niagara Falls (Dunlap 1834, vol. 2, pt. 2, 395). Red Jacket's choice of Niagara Falls may have been a political statement. Niagara Falls would be instantly recognizable to people who saw the portrait, iconographically linking the Seneca to their homelands in western New York. Governor Blacksnake, Red Jacket's cousin and an important traditionalist living at the Allegany Reservation, owned a framed copy of the Weir portrait of Red Jacket that he considered very good (Graymont 1972, 184).

If Red Jacket exercised some control over the production of his painted image, he had bad luck with his image in American letters. The portrait by Weir was the subject of an 1828 poem by Fitz-Greene Halleck, which was very popular when it first appeared and continues to be anthologized in American literature texts. The poem, in utter disregard of the facts, describes Red Jacket as the hereditary king of the Tuscaroras and a fierce warrior (Adkins 1930, 235–40; Wilson 1869, 322–24). Significantly, William L. Stone's 1841 biography of Red Jacket, although not directly contradicting the image left by Halleck's poem, begins by making it clear that Red Jacket was an orator, not a warrior.

The growth of Buffalo and the completion of the Erie Canal brought visitors who were anxious to meet Red Jacket. Local residents, understanding the interest in Red Jacket, recorded their memories of encountering him on the streets of Buffalo. Red Jacket, famous for his speeches, was now transformed into a figure in American folklore.

Red Jacket and the Senecas generally were often portrayed as seriously addicted to drink. Although the Senecas themselves, and Red Jacket in particular, noted the damage that alcohol had done to their nation, the charge must, nevertheless, have seemed particularly galling to Red Jacket, who understood that it was the white people who had brought alcohol to the Indians. Peter B. Porter preserved an anecdote about Red Jacket at the Treaty of Canandaigua in 1794. Pickering had asked for the right to build taverns on the path between the Genesee River and the village of Buffalo. He described the proposed taverns as "walking sticks" that would support travelers on their journeys. Red Jacket responded that such supports would prove to be stumbling blocks to the Indians and rejected the proposal (Porter Papers, Indian Affairs, B-3). The young Millard Fillmore, later president of the United States, recalled seeing Red Jacket for the first time in 1822. Red Jacket showed Fillmore the Washington medal. A few hours later, Fillmore saw the great chief drunk. Other sources say that Red Jacket would pawn the medal when drunk, but always redeemed it (Fillmore, 1879, 13–14; Johnson 1876, 169). Orlando Allen, who knew Red Jacket well in the 1820s, discounted stories of Red Jacket's alcoholism. Although Red Jacket did drink to excess on occasion, he abstained entirely for long periods and never drank when a council was to be held or important business needed to be transacted (Bryant 1879, 351). Similar testimony was given by Major Donald Frasier, who observed Red Jacket while serving with General Porter in the War of 1812. Red Jacket urged the commissary-general not to furnish spirits to his men while engaged in active service and as a matter of principle abstained from liquor during councils (Bryant 1879, 362).

Red Jacket's position among his own people was also a matter of interest. David Eddy, who settled in Erie County in 1804, commented that Red Jacket, although talented, did not appear to be popular among his own people (Turner 1850, 476). A contrasting story is told that when any difficulty occurred on the Caneadea reservation that could not be settled locally, a messenger was sent to Buffalo to lay the problem before Red Jacket, whose decision was "patiently awaited, and generally faithfully carried out" (Minard 1888, 58).

Many people visited Red Jacket in the 1820s, but none more celebrated than General Lafayette, who stopped in Buffalo during his grand tour of the United States in 1825. Both had fought in the Revolutionary War almost fifty years earlier. Lafayette recalled a young warrior he had heard speak at the Treaty of Fort Stanwix in 1784, and Red Jacket said that he was that man. "Time has changed us very much," said Lafayette, "for then we were young and active." Red Jacket rejoined that time had been better for Lafayette, for his face was still smooth and had a head covered with hair. This was not the case with Red Jacket, and he removed the handkerchief covering his head to reveal his bald forehead. An observer at the time commented that Red Jacket appeared to understand English very well but would not reply to Lafayette until his questions were translated into Seneca (Levasseur 1829, 2:209–10). Red Jacket appeared to welcome the attention paid to him by important visitors but maintained his dignity. About 1820 a young French nobleman visiting Buffalo requested that Red Jacket visit him in the City of Buffalo, seven miles from Red Jacket's home. Red Jacket replied to the messenger, "Tell the young man that if he wishes to visit the old chief, he may find him with his nation, where other strangers pay their respects to him, and Red Jacket will be glad to see him" (Stone 1841, 360–61).

9

———

Red Jacket Attacked and Reconciled, 1826–1830

Late in his life, Red Jacket visited "Widow" Berry, an old acquaintance, at Avon, New York. Mrs. Berry asked about his children, and Red Jacket replied: "Red Jacket was once a great man, and in favor with the Great Spirit. He was a lofty pine among the smaller trees of the forest. But after years of glory he degraded himself by drinking the fire-water of the white man. The Great Spirit has looked upon him in anger, and his lightning has stripped the pine of its branches" (Stone 1841, 355).

According to Nathaniel Strong, Red Jacket married twice, first to Waahagadek (World on Fire) at Canawaugus (Avon), and they had thirteen children, all of whom predeceased him. At least some of the children reached adulthood, for Strong reported that in 1863 Red Jacket had three grand-children living on the Cattaraugus Reservation, John Jacket and two women (Strong 1863, 10–11). William Savery, one of the Quaker delegation at the Treaty of Canandaigua in 1794, met Red Jacket's wife and five of his children, whom he described as well clad and "the best behaved and prettiest Indian children I have ever met with" (Savery 1837, 358). Ten or eleven of his children died of consumption (Stone 1841, 354–55).

Arthur Parker was told that Red Jacket had three wives. The first, Wyashoh, died of consumption along with Red Jacket's children. He married again to a younger woman, who soon left him. The last was Degeney, the widow of Chief Two Guns, whom he married in 1820 (1952, 175). The Seneca were beginning to adopt the custom of family names passed on through the male line. Red Jacket's children and grandchildren adopted the last name "Jacket," and Degeney's male children by Two Guns became known as Daniel, Henry, and Lewis Twoguns.

While Red Jacket was fighting the missionaries, his family was joining the new faith. The *American Missionary Register* noted the marriage of Jonathan Jacket, son of Red Jacket, to Yahahweeh in a Christian ceremony (Jan. 1821, 1:280). The same publication also noted, in 1823, the death the previous year of William Jacket, another son of Red Jacket, and of Jonathan Jacket (Feb. 1823, 4:48). In March 1827 Thompson S. Harris, the missionary at Seneca Village at Buffalo Creek, reported that Red Jacket's wife desired to become a Christian even though Red Jacket had told her that if she did so, they must cease being man and wife (*Missionary Herald*, Aug. 1827, 23:248; Harris 1903, 367–69). One of Mrs. Jacket's children, Henry Twoguns, had joined the Seneca Mission Church in 1823 and in 1827 was joined by his mother and his brothers, Lewis and Daniel. The wives of Daniel and Henry Twoguns joined the following year (Harris 1903, 379–80). When his wife became a Christian, Red Jacket left, as threatened, for Tonawanda. Reconciliation came later.

Red Jacket, speaking for the Seneca, had rejected the offers of the Ogden Land Company to purchase the Seneca reservations in 1811 and 1819. The Ogden Land Company was not deterred. On March 2, 1822, David Ogden wrote to the secretary of war, John C. Calhoun, stating that the Christian Party was in favor of the proposed move to Green Bay, but the Pagan Party, with Red Jacket at its head, was opposed (Calhoun 1972, 6:723). Calhoun wrote the following month that the government would endeavor to convince the Indians of the advantages of moving to the west, but no steps would be taken to remove them without their consent (Calhoun 1973, 7:44–45).

In March 1823 Red Jacket, Cornplanter, and Major Berry traveled to Washington where they addressed Calhoun in person. In response to their objections to removing to Green Bay, Calhoun assured them that they could not be compelled to move and were at liberty to follow their own inclinations. But, he continued, it was in their interests to move so as to place distance between themselves and the white settlements. The following day, March 15, 1823, Calhoun wrote to T. L. Ogden, informing him that Red Jacket was opposed to moving and had declared his intention to "live and die on the land he now occupies" (US/SW/IA/LS E:404–7). The Seneca did sell the Gardeau Reservation, the largest of the reservations on the Genesee River, on September 3, 1823. Red Jacket was among the signers of the agreement (Kappler 1904, 2:1033–34).

The difficulties between the Christian and the Pagan Parties over the presence of missionaries on the reservations continued. By 1824 Thomas McKenney, the head of the War Department's new Office of Indian Affairs, was actively opposing Red Jacket. On April 9, 1824, he wrote to Jasper Parrish to condemn the actions of Red Jacket and the Pagan Party, "they being not only hostile to the view of the larger, and more respectable portion of the Six Nations, but also to their own interests, and to the recognized policy of the Government towards them." On December 24, 1824, he wrote directly to the Christian Party, stating, "Your difficulties which Red Jacket has been the chief agent in occasioning, will, it is hoped, all disappear before long" (Calhoun 1974, 9:25–26, 457; US/WD/IA/LS 1:261). As far as Washington was concerned, Red Jacket was no longer the voice of the Seneca but the leader of the backward minority of the nation.

The Ogden Land Company succeeded in convincing the United States government in 1826 that the time had come to make a sale. The Committee on Indian Affairs duly requested the House of Representatives to approve an appropriation for holding a treaty with the Indians in New York. Red Jacket himself was said to be desirous to have a sale of most of the reservations and to have the Indians consolidate on the Allegany Reservation (*Reg. of Debates* 1826, 2:1597). Other congressmen had heard of Red Jacket and were skeptical about his reaction. John Forsyth of Georgia felt that if the question of the disposition of Indian land arose, Red Jacket would lay aside his bottle to oppose it and would never be prevailed upon to give his consent (*Reg. of Debates* 1826, 2:1599). Congressman Michael Hoffman of New York foresaw the probable result:

> Be assured that, whenever your Agent shall go there and propose such a sale, Red Jacket will be ready to meet him, and will drive him from his purpose by arguments which he will find it vain to resist. Sir, it is impossible your Agent should prevail with those Indians against the influence of their favorite Chief. He will call a council, and there he will examine your policy toward the Indian tribes, and your guardianship over them in a manner not very complimentary to this Government. The picture he will there draw before the eyes of his nation, will be by no means flattering. (2:1607)

Despite the skepticism of these congressmen the appropriation for the treaty was made, and in May, Oliver Forward was appointed commissioner. The treaty was held in August 1826, and although Red Jacket raised his objections as predicted, the agreement was signed. Even though Red Jacket had opposed the sale, he insisted on his right to sign as a chief (Stone 1841, 314–15; US/WD/IA/LR, Six Nations

832:235–36, 283–85; *Geneva Palladium,* Sept. 26, 1826; *Niles Weekly Register,* Sept. 16, 1826).

The result of the treaty—if an action that was never ratified by congress is a "treaty"—was the loss of the remaining reservations along the Genesee River, the sale of large tracts from the Buffalo and Tonawanda Reservations, and the same of a smaller tract from Cattaraugus. Only the Allegany and the small Oil Spring Reservations were unchanged.

Although he had signed the treaty, Red Jacket spoke against its ratification. He appealed to the Quakers for assistance, and on May 18, 1827, a delegation from the Indian Committee of New York Yearly Meeting met with representatives of the Seneca Nation in council. At this meeting Red Jacket charged that the Ogden Land Company had bribed the Christian Party but that the Pagan Party always refused to sell, which caused great difficulties between the two. At the treaty itself Oliver Forward, saying he was sent by the Great Father, drew up the articles of sale and told the Indians: "'Tis all one, whether you sign it or not; if you don't your Great Father the President will drive you off, and you will not get a cent for your lands, he will only shew you the way to the Cherokee country" (US/WD/IA/LR, Six Nations 832:227–30).

The Quakers forwarded the allegations to Washington and received in return copies of letters from Oliver Forward and Jasper Parrish responding to Red Jacket's allegations. Parrish, in a letter dated April 20, 1827, claimed that the other chiefs were satisfied with the sale and were angry with Red Jacket for making difficulties for the larger and more respectable part of the nation. In another letter, dated July 6, 1827, Parrish wrote that the dissatisfaction of Red Jacket and others of his party came from the interference of local whites (US/WD/IA/LS 4:108; Society of Friends, NYYM, Indian Committee, Doc., pp. 59–61).

Young King and others of the Christian Party sent a petition to the president on September 13, 1827, disputing an earlier petition by Red Jacket and his party: "Red Jacket is an old man, his mind is broken, his memory is short, and he is devoid of truth. He is not, and never has been the first chief of our Tribe or our Nation. Young King is and has been the first and Great Chief of our Nation" (US/WD/ IA/LR, Six Nations 832:200–202).

Two days later, on September 15, a council met at Buffalo and issued a declaration deposing Red Jacket:

> We, the chiefs of the Seneca tribe, of the Six Nations say to you, Yau-go-ya-yat-haw, (or Red Jacket), that you have for a long time disturbed our councils; that you have procured some white men to assist you in sending a great number of false stories, to our father the president of the United States, and induced our people to sign those falsehoods at Tonawanta [*sic*] as chiefs of our tribe, when you knew that there were not chiefs, that you have opposed the improvement of our nation, and made divisions and disturbances among our people; that you have abused and insulted our great father the president; that you have not regarded the rules which make the Great Spirit love us; and which make his red children do good to each other; that you have a bad heart, because in a time of great distress, when our people were starving, you took and hid a body of a deer you had killed, when your starving brothers should have secured their proportions of it with you; that the last time our father, the president, was fighting against the king, across the great waters, you had divided us, you acted against our father, the president, and his officers, and advised with those who were no friends; that you have prevented, and always discouraged our children from going to school, where they could learn, and abused and lied about our people who were willing to learn, and about those, who were offering to instruct them how to worship the Great Spirit in the manner Christians do; that you have always placed yourself before them, who would be instructed, and have done all you could to prevent their going to school, that you have taken goods to your own use,

which were received as annuities, and which belonged to orphan children, and to old people, that for the last ten years you have often said that the communications from our great father to his red children were forgeries, made up at New York, by those who wished to buy our lands; that you left your wife, because she joined the Christians, and worshipped the Great Spirit as they do, knowing that she was a good woman; that we have waited nearly ten years for you to reform, and do better; but are now discouraged, as you declare you will never receive instruction from those who wish to do us good, as our great father advises, and induced others to hold the same language.

We might say a great many other things, which make you an enemy to the Great Spirit, and also to your own brothers, but we have said enough and now renounce you as a chief, and from this time, you are forbid to act as such—all of our nation will hereafter regard you as a private man, and we say to all of them, that every one who shall do as you have done, if a chief, will in like manner be disowned, and set back were he started from by his brethren.

The document was signed by twenty-six chiefs, headed by Young King, Captain Pollard, and Little Billy (*Niles Weekly Register,* Oct. 6, 1827, 84–85).

One month later, on October 16, 1827, another council was held at the Buffalo Reservation. After the document of the previous month had been read and explained, Levi Halftown rose to give the views of the Cattaraugus Seneca, who were united in their support of Red Jacket. It was then reported that a large majority at Allegany also supported Red Jacket. Big Kettle disputed the specific charges. Red Jacket had not stood in the way of children learning to read but opposed only the teaching of the "black coats" (missionaries) that caused trouble for the Indians. The key issue was land. The Great Spirit had given the land to his Red Children,

Sagoyewatha (Known as Red Jacket).
Portrait by Charles Bird King, c. 1828.
Albright-Knox Art Gallery, Buffalo, New York.
Gift of the Seymour H. Knox Foundation, Inc. 1970.

and George Washington had made it sure. The Great Spirit
had marked out the path, but the Christian Party, listening
to the advice of the white people, "have left this clear path,
and gone among the weeds" (*Niles Weekly Register,* Nov. 3,
1827, 146; *Reformer,* Dec. 1827, 178–80).

Meanwhile, the sale of the land by the Ogden Land Company went forward. The trustees of the Ogden Land Company announced on October 1, 1827, that the land purchased the previous year would go on sale, beginning with the auction of a portion of the Buffalo Reservation on November 15. Title to these lands, said the advertisement, was indisputable (*Geneva Palladium*, Oct. 17, 1827).

Red Jacket and two others traveled to Washington in January 1828 followed by letters to Thomas McKenney from Jasper Parrish and the Christian Party denying that Red Jacket spoke for the Seneca Nation (US/WD/IA/LR, Seneca 808:55–56, 65–66). Red Jacket managed to see President John Quincy Adams on March 7 and 24 and received assurances that an inquiry would be made into the various charges brought by Red Jacket. During his return trip from Washington in March Red Jacket spoke at the Masonic Hall in New York City (Odell 1928, 3:368). His remarks on that occasion are not recorded.

Robert M. Livingston was appointed in May to investigate. He went to Buffalo where he convened a council with the Christian Party, headed by Young King, and the Pagan Party (which Livingston termed the "Diestical Party"), headed by Red Jacket. He invited both sides to substantiate their charges. Red Jacket began with an attack on missionaries. They had promised a schoolmaster, but "the coat of the schoolmaster like that of the Deer, soon changed and he became a preacher." He then turned to the treaty and repeated his story of bribery and corruption (US/WD/IA/LR, Seneca 808:117–20). Captain Pollard and other members of the Christian Party appeared willing to reconcile with Red Jacket. Their own accounts of the negotiations largely supported Red Jacket's assertion that the Indians had been pressured by Commissioner Oliver Forward to sign the treaty (US/WD/IA/LR, Seneca 808:126–32).

Young King spoke for the pro-treaty faction, noting that
even Red Jacket had previously agreed to sales of Seneca
land. The major problem with Red Jacket, however, was his
opposition to all of those, including members of his own
family, who wished to leave off the "old ways" and become
Christian. Tired of Red Jacket's obstructions, Young King
informed Livingston, "We concluded to agree with the President in deposing him" (US/WD/IA/LR, Seneca 808:137–
39). Young King and his faction clearly understood the
opposition to Red Jacket on the part of Jasper Parrish, Thomas
L. McKenney, and the government.

The council concluded on July 4, 1828. Red Jacket said
he was prepared to "look mildly on the past" and admitted
liability to error and promised reformation. He then offered
the deposing decree to Pollard. After some further exchange
between Pollard and Red Jacket, Pollard, Red Jacket, and
Livingston took each others' hands, and Pollard "rent the
decree and cast it on the floor" (US/WD/IA/LR, Seneca
808:167–69).

Livingston wrote to Peter B. Porter, the newly appointed
secretary of war that same day, announcing the reconciliation of the two parties and their agreement for mutual tol-
eration. Porter, Red Jacket's old commander in the War of
1812, was scarcely a disinterested party. He was a major part-
ner in the Ogden Land Company and, thus, would profit
directly from the sale of Seneca lands. Red Jacket, whom
Livingston described as the leader of at least three-fourths of
the nation, had been acknowledged as the "Head Sachem of
the Wolf Tribe," and the Christian party had voluntarily
destroyed their decree deposing Red Jacket. As to the treaty
of 1826, Livingston reported, much evidence had been
collected, but further investigation was required (US/WD/
IA/LR, Six Nations 832:263–64).

Thomas McKenney, in his 1838 sketch of Red Jacket, tells
a much-abbreviated story of Red Jacket's reinstatement. In

McKenney's account Red Jacket's problems are solely the result of his opposition to the missionaries. There is no mention of land. McKenney suggested to Red Jacket that he return home and express in council his willingness to "bury the hatchet" and allow those who chose to be Christians to be so, reserving the right of others to retain the old ways. In McKenney's account this was done, and "as had been promised him at Washington," the council replaced him in office. McKenney made no mention of the issues surrounding the sale of land, the role of his own office in supporting the Christian Party against Red Jacket, the intervention of President Adams, nor the investigation by Livingston (McKenney 1967, 10–11; Manley 1950, 158; see also Stone 1841, 380–86).

Livingston's report went to Secretary of War and Ogden Land Company investor, Peter B. Porter. The Senate vote on the ratification of the treaty on February 29, 1828, was a tie, but on April 8, 1828, the Senate adopted a resolution that their refusal to ratify the treaty was not because of their disapprobation of the terms of the contract but merely "to disclaim the necessity of an interference by the Senate" on the matter. Red Jacket had won a partial victory, but the treaty and sale of 1826 was allowed to stand without further investigation or ratification by the Senate (Manley 1950, 160–62).

With the reconciliation in 1828 between the Christian and Pagan Parties Red Jacket now needed to make peace with his own family. Red Jacket had always spoken for unity and had criticized the missionaries for bringing disunity to the Senecas. The events of the 1820s, both politically and within his own family, had shown that the Christian faction was strong. It would not be possible to drive out the missionaries. What was needed now was peace between the two parties. Red Jacket, for years the symbol of resistance to change, ended his political career working for Seneca unity through reconciliation.

Asher Wright, who followed Thompson S. Harris as missionary to the Senecas, arrived at Buffalo Creek after the death of Red Jacket but was well acquainted with members of the Twogun family and other Senecas who had known Red Jacket well. In 1852 Wright wrote a long letter to the *Buffalo Commercial Advertiser* (Apr. 15, 1852) to counter claims that Red Jacket had died an unreconstructed enemy of the Christians. Although Mrs. Jacket had been firm in her resolve to become a Christian, she wanted Red Jacket to return, so William Jones, a relative of Red Jacket's and a member of the Wolf Clan, went to Tonawanda to ask him to return. Red Jacket said that he would think it over and a few days later came back to Buffalo as if nothing had happened. For some time after, he would leave his house on Sundays but later would stay and look after the house while his wife was at church.

Ruth Stevenson, Red Jacket's stepdaughter, later recalled how they used to eat their meals on the floor of their cabin or in warm weather outside on the ground. Once, when a group of white people were coming to see Red Jacket, Mrs. Jacket was embarrassed and got up to leave. Red Jacket told her to stay as there was no shame in what they did, but Mrs. Jacket retired from the scene. A few days later, Red Jacket walked to Buffalo and returned at sundown carrying a large cherry-wood dining table on his back, which he presented to his wife, saying "Now, Mother, we can eat like the white folks" (BHS 1885, 100).

In Asher Wright's account Red Jacket sent for the missionary Thompson Harris a short time before his death to apologize for his former behavior: "What the minister said was right, I abused him—he compared me to a snake slyly trying to bite someone. This is very true, and I wish to repent and make satisfaction" (*Buffalo Commercial Advertiser,* Apr. 15, 1852). Harris was away and did not reach Red Jacket's house until after Red Jacket's death. On another

Houses of Red Jacket and William Jones
at the Buffalo Creek Reservation, ca. 1830.
From William L. Stone, *Life and Times of Red-Jacket* (1841).

occasion Red Jacket told an old acquaintance that he no longer hated the Christians but had spoken so often against it that he was ashamed to go back.

In July 1827 Abel Bingham, the Baptist missionary at Tonawanda whom Red Jacket had attempted to eject in 1822, encountered Red Jacket on the road, and the two had a long conversation on religion. Red Jacket repeated his objections to ministers although he acknowledged Bingham to be a good man. Bingham wanted to turn the interview to the subject of Red Jacket's own end and, after what Bingham described as a long and pleasant interview, suggested that they pray that the Lord would prepare Red Jacket for a peaceful and happy death. Red Jacket deferred, at least until the proposed prayer could be translated, but a few days later at a second meeting thanked the missionary for his friendly talk and said it had made a deep impression upon him (Cumming 1979, 191–93).

Red Jacket made one last trip. From January through April 1829 Red Jacket spoke in theaters and lecture halls in Albany, New York City, Washington, and Boston. He appeared at the American Museum and Peale's Museum in New York City, sometimes in connection with other entertainments. An editorial in the *Catskill Recorder* (as reprinted in the *Albany Argus,* Feb. 19, 1829) lamented the decline of Red Jacket, who twenty years earlier would have scorned paid appearances. The old Red Jacket would not have allowed the "sacred dances" of his tribe to be exhibited where they would be stared at by "curious and sneering strangers." William L. Stone commented that Red Jacket had "become so lost to the pride of character, as to allow the keepers of museums . . . to exhibit him for money" (Stone 1841, 389).

Whatever other motives Red Jacket had, whether fame or money, he also had a political purpose. He was traveling to Washington to see the newly elected president, Andrew Jackson. What passed between Red Jacket and Jackson is unclear. Newspaper advertisements for his "long talks" at the American Museum in New York City in early March 1829 promised that Red Jacket would relate the substance of his conversation with the new president. The advertisement in the March 5, 1829, issue of the *New York Evening Post* said that he would also discuss his complaint against the former government and the promises of the new government.

Although the newspapers heavily advertised Red Jacket's appearances, none seems to have reported Red Jacket's actual words. An obituary, published in the *New York Spectator* (Jan. 27, 1830) at the time of Red Jacket's death, refers to one of Red Jacket's final speeches as giving "a parallel between Washington and Jackson, which was admirably sketched, and abounded with nice discriminations of character. He appeared to possess an accurate knowledge of the character, temper, talents, and dispositions of both." William L. Stone gives an account of one of Red Jacket's final speeches in

Albany. The New York State legislature was in session, and the audience was filled with Jackson supporters, who somehow had the impression that Red Jacket was an admirer of the new president and were quite unhappy when Red Jacket contrasted Washington and Jackson "greatly to the disadvantage of the latter." Stone describes the speech as "feeble and puerile" (Stone 1841, 389–90).

The transition from President John Quincy Adams to President Andrew Jackson did not bode well for Red Jacket's aim of preserving Seneca lands in New York. Thomas L. McKenney, the Superintendent of Indian Affairs, was deposed from office. McKenney had supported the Christian Party against Red Jacket but did also seem to have been genuinely concerned for the welfare of the Indians. Red Jacket had good reason to think that the political situation had gotten worse, not only for the Seneca but for all Indians east of the Mississippi.

While in Washington Red Jacket stopped in to see outgoing President John Quincy Adams. He told Adams that they were both old and that he would soon be called for by the Great Spirit. Adams responded that it was true and that he hoped it would be for a better world (Nevins 1928, 387–88). On the same trip Red Jacket visited Rev. John Breckenridge at Baltimore. He and Breckenridge had discussed religion and missionaries at Buffalo in 1821, and, although they disagreed, they were on friendly terms. Red Jacket's opposition to the missionaries never prevented him from having good relations with missionaries and other whites he believed were sincere and concerned with the welfare of the Indians. Breckenridge described Red Jacket as dejected and forlorn and aware of his approaching death (Stone 1841, 336–52). Red Jacket was making his final peace with his former adversaries.

Red Jacket's final political act was to call a council to reunite the Christian and Pagan Parties. The council was sitting at the time of Red Jacket's death (*Missionary Herald,* Apr. 1830, 26:116–19; Stone 1841, 392–93; Parker 1952, 203–6).

Red Jacket died on January 20, 1830, and was buried in the cemetery near the Seneca mission. There are three variations of the conduct at Red Jacket's funeral. According to the missionary, Thompson S. Harris, Red Jacket had left the management of his burial to his wife's son-in-law (William Jones) and to the Wolf Clan. The funeral was held in the mission church, much to the disappointment of some white "infidels" (Harris's word) who came hoping to see a pagan funeral (*Rochester Observer,* Apr. 30, 1830; Stone 1841, 394). Other accounts agree that the funeral was held in the mission church but that Red Jacket was first eulogized by chiefs of the Pagan Party, "who seemed indifferent to all the religious services which followed" (*Rochester Daily Advertiser and Telegraph,* Jan. 26, 1830; *Rochester Gem,* Feb. 6, 1830, 157).

The final version of the funeral has Red Jacket telling his friends that he wanted to be buried following the old customs. "Be sure that my grave be not made by a white man; let them not pursue me there!" In this version the missionary blatantly disregards Red Jacket's final wishes and is rebuked during the funeral by a chief named Green Blanket. The "pagans" refused to follow Red Jacket to the mission cemetery (McKenney 1967, 10–13; *Buffalo Commercial Advertiser,* Apr. 3, 1852). In yet another version Red Jacket tells his daughter that when he dies, the white man will ask for his body, but he wishes to be buried with his own people. "The missionary who has come here says the dead will rise; perhaps they will; if they do, I wish to rise with my Indian friends. I do not wish to rise among pale faces. I wish to be surrounded by red men" (Caswell 1892, 273–74).

Asher Wright, who worked as a missionary at Buffalo Creek Reservation from 1831 to 1845 and then at Cattaraugus Reservation until his death in 1875, knew Red Jacket's widow and stepchildren well. By Wright's account, based on the testimony of Red Jacket's family, Red Jacket regretted his former conduct toward missionaries and wished to make peace. Red Jacket committed his remains to his family, charging them to manage the funeral in their own way (*Buffalo Commercial Advertiser,* Apr. 15, 1852). This version of events is supported by manuscript accounts of Red Jacket's last days by Nicholson Parker and/or Ely Parker in the Parker family papers at the Buffalo and Erie County Historical Society (Parker Family Papers, BHS, folders 3–4).

Ten days after Red Jacket's death, a "dead feast" was held, and there it was proclaimed that Red Jacket's medal that he had received from George Washington in 1792 would be given to Jemmy Johnson (Sosehawa), a nephew of Red Jacket and the grandson of Handsome Lake. The medal was later given to Ely S. Parker in 1851 when Parker became a sachem (*Buffalo Commercial Advertiser,* Nov. 26, 1896; *Geneva Gazette,* Mar. 13, 1891; Armstrong 1974; Severance 1921, 241–42; BHS 1885, 101). This medal is now in the possession of the Buffalo and Erie County Historical Society.

In his final years, beset by the Ogden Land Company, the policies of the United States government, and the Pagan Party, Red Jacket sometimes felt that he alone stood between the Seneca and the loss of their lands. Mary Burt, the sister of Pascal Pratt, told the story of how Red Jacket once fell through the ice of Buffalo Creek near the Pratt house. He called to Pascal Pratt to "come and help Jack out, if you don't the black coats [missionaries] will get all the land" (Letchworth 1874, 89).

Although Red Jacket died in January 1830, he was not silenced. The distribution of his speeches had made his word part of the American political vocabulary. When the issue of Cherokee removal was before Congress in 1830, a congressman from Tennessee named David Crockett quoted Red Jacket to oppose the Jacksonian policy of Indian removal (Jahoda 1971, 65; Shackford 1956, 116, 304). During the

Cherokee removal controversy a short pamphlet appeared, attributed to Red Jacket, titled *First Impressions on Reading the Message of the Governor of Georgia, 1830, Relative to the Indians,* which reviewed the legal issues of Indian land ownership and the relations between Indians and the United States government. Although the pamphlet is clearly not written by Red Jacket, it invokes his name, and its closing arguments about the moral rights of the Indian to fair treatment show a familiarity with the style and arguments made again and again by Red Jacket.

Red Jacket's legacy did not save the Buffalo Creek Reservation. The Ogden Land Company continued its attempt to purchase the remaining reservations of the Six Nations. On January 15, 1838, the Treaty of Buffalo Creek was signed. All of the Indians of New York were to remove west of the Mississippi to the Indian Territory. The Senecas would receive $202,000 for the land. The treaty was widely regarded as a fraud, and the antiemigration part of the Seneca, aided by Quakers and other whites, lobbied against the ratification of the treaty. A second treaty, signed May 20, 1842, returned to the Seneca the Cattaraugus and Allegany Reservations, but Ogden and Fellows would retain the Buffalo Creek and Tonawanda Reservations. Over the next several years the Indians on the Buffalo Creek Reservation left for Cattaraugus and Allegany. The Seneca at Tonawanda refused to accept either the original 1838 treaty or the compromise treaty of 1842. They had signed neither and remained on their land. Their right to the land was recognized by a new treaty in 1857, which restored most of the land claimed by the Ogden Land Company under the earlier treaties (Pedersen 1956, 7–10).

In 1837 an actor named Henry Placade arranged for Red Jacket's grave at the burial grounds near the Seneca Mission Church to be marked with a marble slab. Thomas McKenney was among those who attended its dedication (*Army and Navy Chronicle,* Sept. 7, 1837). Visitors to the grave site chipped away pieces of the marker for souvenirs (*Buffalo Daily Courier*, Feb. 27, 1851).

With the sale of the Buffalo Reservation the Seneca began leaving their old homes for Cattaraugus and Allegany Reservations. The Ogden Land Company promised that the Buffalo Mission Church and the burial ground would remain in the possession and control of the Seneca Nation (BHS 1885, 54; *Buffalo Express,* Mar. 14, 1897). The Mission Church and the burial grounds fell into disrepair, and, in 1851, there were suggestions that the famous Red Jacket be moved to the new Forest Lawn Cemetery in Buffalo (*Buffalo Daily Courier,* Feb. 21, 1851; *Buffalo Commercial Advertiser,* Mar. 3–5, 31, 1851).

In March 1852 George Copeway, a Chippewa from Canada, lectured in Buffalo on the "Religion, Poetry and Eloquence of the Indians." Copeway solicited funds for a memorial to Red Jacket. In response, Dr. Peter Wilson, a Cayuga living on the Cattaraugus Reservation, delivered a brief but eloquent address in which he told his audience that Red Jacket had said in his final illness: "Be sure that my grave is not made by a white man—let them not pursue me there." He then told the audience that Red Jacket's friends would soon take away Red Jacket's remains to the Cattaraugus Reservation (*Buffalo Commercial Adv*ertiser, Mar. 17, 18, 1852, Mar. 15, 1860; *Buffalo Daily Commercial,* Mar. 18, 1852).

Although Copeway's appeal and Peter Wilson's response were published in the newspapers at that time, the full story of Copeway's actions was not made public until years later. Ely Parker later told how Copeway, along with a local businessman named Wheeler Hotchkiss and an undertaker named Farrell, had already disinterred Red Jacket and his bones now lay in the basement of Hotchkiss's residence. Some Senecas were still living on the old Buffalo Creek Reservation, including Moses Stevenson (the brother-in-law of Ruth Stevenson, Red Jacket's stepdaughter), Daniel Twoguns, and

Thomas Jemison. Stevenson and Twoguns, with a crowd of sympathetic whites, went to Hotchkiss and demanded the return of the bones, which were then taken to the Cattaraugus Reservation and given to Ruth Stevenson (BHS 1885, 62–63). In another variation of the story Moses Stevenson and Twoguns went to Hugh Cameron, a local lawyer, for advice. They told Cameron that Copeway has stolen the bones and intended to illustrate his lecture with the skull of Red Jacket. Cameron provided the legal advice but then advised them not to wait for legal action but to go as quietly as possible, break down the door if necessary, and be out of town with the skeleton as quickly as possible (Simms 1883, 2:71).

After 1852 Red Jacket's bones were hidden on the Cattaraugus Reservation. The idea of removing Red Jacket's remains to Forest Lawn was revived again in 1860 and 1863. Finally, in 1876 William C. Bryant of the Buffalo Historical Society received approval from the Seneca Nation for the reburial at Forest Lawn. Red Jacket's remains were taken to Buffalo where they were kept in a bank vault until the site could be prepared.

The remains of Young King, Captain Pollard (with his wife and grandchild), Destroy-Town, Little Billy, Tall Peter, and several other unidentified Indians were also removed from the old mission cemetery to be reinterred with Red Jacket at Forest Lawn. The bones of Farmer's Brother, who died in 1814 and was buried in Buffalo, had been moved to Forest Lawn in 1852. In his final resting place Red Jacket was reunited with his old companions, including the leaders of the Christian Party who had opposed him in the 1820s and with whom he reconciled in 1828.

The bones were reinterred at Forest Lawn on October 9, 1884. The ceremony was attended by representatives of the Six Nations from New York and Canada, including two grandchildren of Red Jacket, John Jacket (Sho-gyo-a-ja-ach) and Abby Jacket (Oh-no-syo-dyno). The major addresses at the occasion were delivered by William C. Bryant of the Buffalo Historical Society and Ely S. Parker (BHS 1885, 11-46). On June 22, 1892, a monument and statue of Red Jacket were dedicated at Forest Lawn. The honor of unveiling was given to John Jacket, described as the grandson and last surviving descendant in a direct line from Red Jacket (BHS 1893, 23). Red Jacket's birthplace at Canoga, New York, had been marked with a memorial erected by the Waterloo Library and Historical Society in 1891 (Waterloo 1892). In 1894 more remains from the old burial ground were moved to Forest Lawn.

By the last decade of Red Jacket's life Americans in the east were beginning to grow nostalgic about the Indian. James Fenimore Cooper's *Last of the Mohicans* was published in 1826. When Red Jacket died, his obituary in *Niles Weekly Register* (Feb. 13, 1830, 411) called him the "last of the Senecas." Thomas McKenney, in his 1838 sketch, wrote that with Red Jacket had died "all that remained of the spirit of his tribe" (McKenney 1967, 1).

Red Jacket was the last active and visible member of the generation of Senecas who could recall the power of the Iroquois Confederacy before the American Revolution when representatives of both the British and Americans sought to gain their allegiance. Cornplanter did not die until March 1836, but he had withdrawn from active political life. Jasper Parrish and Horatio Jones also died in 1836. Governor Blacksnake, Red Jacket's cousin and perhaps the last survivor of that generation, died at an advanced age in 1859. By 1830 the Senecas had been on the reservations for thirty years, and only the middle-aged and older people could remember when their lands stretched unbroken from the Finger Lakes and Genesee Valley to the far west of the state, and the influence of the Six Nations extended far into the Ohio country. At the time William L. Stone's biography of Red Jacket was published in 1841, it seemed apparent that, as a consequence of the Treaty of 1838, all of the Seneca would leave New York State for the west.

But the Seneca Nation and the Tonawanda Band of Seneca did not leave. The majority desired to retain their old homes and worked to overturn (or, in the end, modify) the Treaty of 1838. No single voice matched that of Red Jacket, but younger men such as Maris Pierce and Peter Wilson spoke forcefully for the Seneca and Cayuga in defense of their lands during the 1830s and 1840s. It should also be said that Nathaniel Strong, the son of Captain Strong, was an able advocate for the proemigration party in this controversy.

Red Jacket is largely known through his speeches to the Reverend Cram (1805) and the Reverend Alexander (1811). The speech against Cram, is perhaps, the most widely reprinted work of a Native American author and continues to be printed and circulated. In these speeches and elsewhere Red Jacket makes a positive claim for the essential morality and religiosity of traditional culture and defends the Native Americans' claim to their lands.

Red Jacket was the defender of Indian land. He may have accepted the inevitability that the Six Nations and the Seneca would lose the bulk of their vast territory to the greed of land speculators and the desire of the white settlers for more farmland. His opposition to the sales in the 1780s and 1790s may have been at least partially a bargaining position, but after 1802, Red Jacket became increasingly unwilling to yield any additional territory, particularly the Buffalo Reservation. The loss of the Genesee Reservations in 1823 and 1826, the loss of large portions of the Buffalo Creek and Tonawanda Reservations in 1826, and the loss of Buffalo in 1842 (after Red Jacket's death) were defeats for Red Jacket, but the ultimate retention of the Cattaraugus, Allegany, and Tonawanda Reservations should be seen as part of Red Jacket's legacy. The fact that the bulk of the Senecas remained in

New York, rather than moving to the west or into Canada, is also part of the Red Jacket legacy.

The Treaty of Canandaigua in 1794, which sets out the basis for the relationship between the United States and the Indians in New York State, is in large measure the result of negotiations between Timothy Pickering and Red Jacket from 1790 to 1794. The treaty is still in effect although disputes between the Iroquois, New York State, and the United States government on the nature of Iroquois sovereignty have also persisted for more than two centuries with little apparent chance of final settlement.

Red Jacket was the defender of Indian sovereignty and independence in the Stiff-Armed George trial in 1801–2 and in the Tommy-Jemmy trial in 1821. Again, Red Jacket was partially defeated by New York State's extension of jurisdiction over the Seneca within the state boundaries, but Red Jacket's arguments remain to counterbalance the claims of the state.

Appendixes
Bibliography
Index

APPENDIX A

Treaty of Fort Stanwix, 1784

Articles of a Treaty conducted at fort Stanwix, on the twenty-second day of October, one thousand seven hundred and eighty-four, between Oliver Wolcott, Richard Butler, and Arthur Lee, commissioners plenipotentiary from the United States in Congress assembled, on the one part, and the sachems and Warriors of the Six Nations, on the other.

The United States of America give peace to the Senecas, Mohawks, Onondagas and Cayugas, and receive them into their protection, upon the following conditions.

ARTICLE 1. Six hostages shall be immediately delivered to the commissioners by the said nations, to remain in possession of the United States, till all the prisoners, white and black, which were taken by said Senecas, Mohawks, Onondagas, and Cayugas, or by any of them, in the late war, from among the people of the United States, shall be delivered up.

ARTICLE 2. The Oneida and Tuscarora nations shall be secured in the possession of the lands on which they are settled.

ARTICLE 3. A line shall be drawn, beginning at the mouth of a creek about four miles east of Niagara, called Oyonwayea, or Johnston's Landing-Place, upon the lake named by the Indians Oswego, and by us Ontario; from thence southerly, in a direction always four miles east of the carrying-path, between lakes Erie and Ontario, to the mouth of Tehoseroron or Buffaloe creek, on Lake Erie; thence south to the north boundary of the State of

Reprinted from *American State Papers. Indian Affairs* (1832), vol. 1, p. 10.

Pennsylvania; thence west, to the end of the said north boundary; thence south along the west boundary of the said State, to the river Ohio; the said line, from the mouth of the Oyonwayea to the Ohio, shall be the western boundary of the lands of the Six Nations; so that the Six Nations shall and do yield to the United States, all claims to the country west of said boundary; and then they shall be secured in the peaceful possession of the lands they inhabit, east and north of the same, reserving only six miles square round the fort of Oswego, to the United States, for the support of the same.

ARTICLE 4. The Commissioners of the United States, in consideration of the present circumstances of the Six Nations, and in execution of the humane and liberal views of the United States, upon the signing of the above articles, will order goods to be delivered to the said Six Nations for their use and comfort.

OLIVER WOLCOTT,
RICHARD BUTLER,
ARTHUR LEE.

[Signed by the sachems and warriors of the Mohawk, Onondaga, Seneca, Oneida, Cayuga, Tuscarora, and Seneca Abeal tribes of Indians.]

APPENDIX B

Treaty of Canandaigua, 1794

A Treaty between the United States of America and the Tribes of Indians called the Six Nations.

The President of the United States having determined to hold a conference with the Six Nations of Indians, for the purpose of removing from their minds all causes of complaint, and establishing a firm and permanent friendship with them; and Timothy Pickering being appointed sole agent for that purpose; and the agent having met and conferred with the sachems, chiefs and warriors of the Six Nations, in a general council: Now, in order to accomplish the good design of this conference, the parties have agreed on the following articles; which, when ratified by the President, with the advice and consent of the Senate of the United States, shall be binding on them and the Six Nations.

ARTICLE 1. Peace and friendship are hereby firmly established, and shall be perpetual between the United States and the Six Nations.

ARTICLE 2. The United States acknowledge the lands reserved to the Oneida, Onondaga and Cayuga Nations, in their respective treaties with the state of New-York, and called their reservations, to be their property; and the United States will never claim the same, nor disturb them or either of the Six Nations, nor their Indian friends residing thereon and united with them, in the free

Reprinted from *American State Papers. Indian Affairs* (1832), Vol. 1, p. 545.

use and enjoyment thereof; but the said reservations shall remain theirs, until they choose to sell the same to the people of the United States, who have the right to purchase.

ARTICLE 3. The land of the Seneca nation is bounded as follows: beginning on Lake Ontario at the northwest corner of the land they sold to Oliver Phelps; the line runs westerly along the lake, as far as Oyongwongyeh creek, at Johnston's Landing place, about four miles eastward from the fort of Niagara; then, southerly, up that creek to its main fork; then straight to the main fork of Stedman's creek, which empties into the river Niagara, above fort Schlosser; and then onward, from that fork, continuing the same straight course, to that river; (this line, from the mouth of Oyongwongyeh creek to the river Niagara, about Fort Schlosser; being the eastern boundary of a strip of land, extending from the same to Niagara river, which the Seneca nation ceded to the King of Great-Britain, at a treaty held about thirty years ago, with Sir William Johnson; then the line runs along the river Niagara to Lake Erie; then along Lake Erie, to the northeast corner of a triangular piece of land, which the United States conveyed to the State of Pennsylvania, as by the President's patent, dated the third day of March, 1792; then due south to the northern boundary of that state; then due east to the southwest corner of the land sold by the Seneca nation to Oliver Phelps; and then north and northerly, along Phelps's line, to the place of beginning, on Lake Ontario. Now, the United States acknowledge all the land within the aforementioned boundaries, to be the property of the Seneca nation; and the United States will never claim the same, nor disturb the Seneca nation, nor any of the Six Nations, or of their Indian friends residing thereon and united with them, in the free use and enjoyment thereof; but it shall remain theirs, until they choose to sell the same to the people of the United States, who have a right to purchase.

ARTICLE 4. The United States having thus described and acknowledged what lands belong to the Oneidas, Onondagas, Cayugas, and Senecas, and engaged never to claim the same, nor disturb them, or any of the Six Nations, or their Indian friends residing thereon and united with them, in the free use and enjoyment thereof: now, the Six Nations, and each of them, hereby engage that they will never claim any other lands within the boundaries of the United States; nor ever disturb the people of the United States in the free use and enjoyment thereof.

ARTICLE 5. The Seneca nation, all others of the Six Nations concurring, cede to the United States the right of making a wagon road from fort Schlosser to Lake Erie, as far south as Buffalo creek; and the people of the United States shall have the free and undisturbed use of this road, for the purposes of travelling and transportation. And the Six Nations, and each of them, will forever allow to the people of the United States, a free passage through their lands, and the free use of the harbors and rivers, adjoining and within their respective tracts of land, for the passing and securing of vessels and boats, and liberty to land their cargoes, where necessary, for their safety.

ARTICLE 6. In consideration of the peace and friendship hereby established, and of the engagements entered into by the Six Nations; and because the United States desire, with humanity and kindness, to contribute to their comfortable support; and to render the peace and friendship hereby established strong and perpetual; the United States now deliver to the Six Nations, and the Indians of the other nations residing among, and united with them, a quantity of goods of the value of ten thousand dollars. And for the same considerations, and with a view to promote the future welfare of the Six Nations, and of their Indian friends aforesaid, the United States will add the sum of three thousand dollars to the one thousand five hundred dollars heretofore allowed them by an article ratified by the President, on the twentythird day of April, 1792, making in the whole, four thousand five hundred dollars; which shall be expended yearly, forever, in purchasing clothing, domestic animals, implements of husbandry, and other utensils, suited to their circumstances, and in compensating useful artificers, who shall reside with or near them, and be employed for their benefit. The immediate application of the whole allowance now stipulated, to be made by the superintendent appointed by the President, for the affairs of the Six Nations and their Indian friends aforesaid.

ARTICLE 7. Lest the firm peace and friendship now established should be interrupted by the misconduct of individuals, the United States and Six Nations agree, that, for injuries done by individuals, on either side, no private revenge or retaliation shall take place; but, instead thereof, complaint shall be made by the party injured, to the other: by the Six Nations, or any of them, to the President of the United States, or the superintendent by him appointed; and by the superintendent, or other person appointed by the President, to the principal chiefs of the Six Nations, or of the nation to which the offender belongs: and such prudent measures shall then be pursued, as shall be necessary to preserve our peace and friendship unbroken; until the legislature (or great council) of the United States shall make other equitable provision for the purpose.

Note: It is clearly understood by the parties to this treaty, that the annuity, stipulated in the sixth article, is to be applied to the benefit of the Six Nations, and of their Indian friends united with them, as aforesaid, as do or shall reside within the boundaries of the United States; For the United States do not interfere with nations, tribes, or families of Indians elsewhere resident.

In witness whereof, the said Timothy Pickering, and the sachems and war chiefs of the said Six Nations, have hereunto set their hands and seals.

Done at Canandaigua, in the State of New York, the eleventh day of November, in the year one thousand seven hundred and ninety-four.

TIMOTHY PICKERING.

[Signed by fifty-nine sachems and war chiefs of the Six Nations.]

APPENDIX C

Red Jacket's Reply to Reverend Cram, 1805

INDIAN SPEECH.

[In the summer of 1805, a number of the principal Chiefs and Warriors of the Six Nations of Indians, principally Senecas, assembled at Buffalo Creek, in the State of New-York, at the particular request of a gentleman Missionary from the State of Massachusetts.* The Missionary being furnished with an Interpreter, and accompanied by the Agent of the United States for Indian affairs, met the Indians in Council, when the following talk took place.]

FIRST, BY THE AGENT.

"Brothers of the Six Nations; I rejoice to meet you at this time, and thank the Great Spirit, that he has preserved you in health, and given me another opportunity of taking you by the hand.

This speech has been reprinted many times, and numerous minor variations and additions appear in the text (Robie 1986; Densmore 1987). The first known edition, from which all other later printings appear to derive, was published in the *Monthly Anthology and Boston Review* in April 1809 (6:221–24). The present text is as first published in 1809.

* Reverend Cram.

"Brothers; The person who sits by me, is a friend who has come a great distance to hold a talk with you. He will inform you what his business is, and it is my request that you would listen with attention to his words."

MISSIONARY. "My Friends; I am thankful for the opportunity afforded us of uniting together at this time. I had a great desire to see you, and inquire into your state and welfare; for this purpose I have travelled a great distance, being sent by your old friends, the Boston Missionary Society. You will recollect they formerly sent missionaries among you, to instruct you in religion, and labour for your good. Although they have not heard from you for a long time, yet they have not forgotten their brothers the Six Nations, and are still anxious to do you good.

"Brothers: I have not come to get your lands or your money, but to enlighten your minds, and to instruct you how to worship the Great Spirit agreeably to his mind and will, and to preach to you the gospel of his son Jesus Christ. There is but one true religion, and but one way to serve God, and if you do not embrace the right way, you cannot be happy hereafter. You have never worshipped the Great Spirit in a manner acceptable to him; but have all your lives been in great errours [sic] and darkness. To endeavour to remove these errours, and open your eyes, so that you might see clearly, is my business with you.

"Brothers: I wish to talk with you as one friend talks with another; and if you have any objections to receive the religion which I preach, I wish you to state them; and I will endeavour to satisfy your minds, and remove the objections.

"Brothers: I want you to speak your minds freely; for I wish to reason with you on the subject, and, if possible, remove all doubts, if there be any on your minds. The subject is an important one, and it is of consequence that you give it an early attention while the offer is made you. Your friends, the Boston Missionary Society, will continue to send you good and faithful ministers, to instruct and strengthen you in religion, if, on your part, you are willing to receive them.

"Brothers; Since I have been in this part of the country, I have visited some of your small villages, and talked with your people.

They appear willing to receive instruction, but, as they look up to you as their older brothers in council, they first want to know your opinion on the subject.

"You have now heard what I have to propose at present. I hope you will take it into consideration, and give me an answer before we part."

After about two hours consultation among themselves, the Chief commonly called by the white people, Red Jacket,★ rose and spoke as follows:

"Friend and Brother; It was the will of the Great Spirit that we should meet together this day. He orders all things, and has given us a fine day for our Council. He has taken his garment from before the sun, and caused it to shine with brightness upon us. Our eyes are opened, that we see clearly; our ears are unstopped, that we have been able to hear distinctly the words you have spoken. For all these favors we thank the Great Spirit; and Him only.

"Brother; This council fire was kindled by you. It was at your request that we came together at this time. We have listened with attention to what you have said. You requested us to speak our minds freely. This gives us great joy; for we now consider that we stand upright before you, and can speak what we think. All have heard your voice, and all speak to you now as one man. Our minds have agreed.

"Brother; You say you want an answer to your talk before you leave this place. It is right you should have one, as you are a great distance from home, and we do not wish to detain you. But we will first look back a little, and tell you what our fathers have told us, and what we have heard from the white people.

"Brother; Listen to what we say.

"There was a time when our forefathers owned this great island. Their seats extended from the rising to the setting sun. The Great Spirit had made it for the use of Indians. He had created the buffalo, the deer, and other animals for food. He had made the

★ His Indian name is Sagu-yu-what-ha; which interpreted is, Keeper awake.

bear and the beaver. Their skins served us for clothing. He had
scattered them over the country, and taught us how to take them.
He had caused the earth to produce corn for bread. All this He
had done for his red children, because He loved them. If we had
some disputes about our hunting ground, they were generally
settled without the shedding of much blood. But an evil day came
upon us. Your forefathers crossed the great water, and landed on
this island. Their numbers were small. They found friends and not
enemies. They told us they had fled from their own country for
fear of wicked men, and had come here to enjoy their religion.
They asked for a small seat. We took pity on them, granted their
request; and they sat down amongst us. We gave them corn and
meat, they gave us poison (alluding, it is supposed, to ardent
spirits) in return.

"The white people had now found our country. Tidings were
carried back, and more came amongst us. Yet we did not fear them.
We took them to be friends. They called us brothers. We believed
them, and gave them a larger seat. At length their numbers had
greatly increased. They wanted more land; they wanted our country. Our eyes were opened, and our minds became uneasy. Wars
took place. Indians were hired to fight against Indians, and many
of our people were destroyed. They also brought strong liquor
amongst us. It was strong and powerful, and has slain thousands.

"Brother; Our seats were once large and yours were small. You
have now become a great people, and we have scarcely a place left
to spread our blankets. You have got our country, but are not
satisfied; you want to force your religion upon us.

"Brother; Continue to listen.

"You say that you are sent to instruct us how to worship the
Great Spirit agreeably to his mind, and, if we do not take hold of
the religion which you white people teach, we shall be unhappy
hereafter. You say that you are right and we are lost. How do we
know this to be true? We understand that your religion is written
in a book. If it was intended for us as well as you, why has not
the Great Spirit given to us, and not only to us, but why did he
not give to our forefathers the knowledge of that book, with the
means of understanding it rightly? We only know what you tell

us about it. How shall we know when to believe, being so often deceived by the white people?

"Brother; You say there is but one way to worship and serve the Great Spirit. If there is but one religion; why do you white people differ so much about it? Why not all agreed, as you can all read the book?

"Brother; We do not understand these things.

"We are told that your religion was given to your forefathers, and has been handed down from father to son. We also have a religion, which was given to our forefathers, and has been handed down to us their children. We worship in that way. It teaches us to be thankful for all the favors we receive; to love each other, and to be united. We never quarrel about religion.

"Brother; The Great Spirit has made us all, but he has made a great difference between his white and red children. He has given us different complexions and different customs. To you He has given the arts. To these He has not opened our eyes. We know these things to be true. Since He has made so great a difference between us in other things; why may we not conclude that He has given us a different religion according to our understanding? The Great Spirit does right. He knows what is best for his children; we are satisfied.

"Brother; We do not wish to destroy your religion or take it from you. We only want to enjoy our own.

"Brother; We are told that you have been preaching to white people in this place. These people are our neighbors. We are acquainted with them. We will wait a little while, and see what effect your preaching has upon them. If we find it does them good, makes them honest, and less disposed to cheat Indians; we will then consider again of what you have said.

"Brother; You have now heard our answer to your talk, and this is all we have to say at present.

"As we are going to part, we will come and take you by the hand, and hope the Great Spirit will protect you on your journey, and return you safe to your friends."

As the Indians began to approach the missionary, he rose hastily from his seat and replied, that he could not take them by the hand; that there was no fellowship between the religion of God and the works of the devil.

This being interpreted to the Indians, they smiled, and retired in a peaceable manner.

It being afterwards suggested to the missionary that his reply to the Indians was rather indiscreet; he observed, that he supposed the ceremony of shaking hands would be received by them as a token that he assented to what was said. Being otherwise informed, he said he was very sorry for the expressions.

Red Jacket to Reverend John Alexander, 1811

Speech of Red Jacket, called by the Indians, Sa-gu-yu-what-hah, or Keeper awake.

In answer to a Speech of the Rev. Mr. Alexander, a missionary from the Missionary Society in New York, to the Seneca Nation of Indians, delivered at a Council, held at Buffalo Creek in May, 1811.

"Brother—We listened to the talk you delivered to us from the Council of black coats★ in New York. We have fully considered your talk, and the offers you have made us; we perfectly understand them, and we return an answer which we wish you also to understand. In making up our minds we have looked back and remembered what has been done in our days, and what our fathers have told us was done in the old times.

"Brother—Great numbers of black coats have been amongst the Indians, and with sweet voices, and smiling faces, have offered to teach them the religion of the white people. Our brethren in

---

Red Jacket's two speeches at a council held in Buffalo in May 1811, the first to Mr. Richardson, an agent of the Ogden Land Company, and the second to Rev. John Alexander, of the New York Missionary Society, were first published at Canandaigua, New York, in a pamphlet titled *Native Eloquence* and have been frequently reprinted. The following text is taken from the *American Speaker* (1816), pages 378-79.

★The appellation given to the clergymen by the Indians.

the East listened to the black coats—turned from the religion of
their fathers, and took up the religion of the white people. What
good has it done them? Are they more happy and more friendly
one to another than we are? No, brother, they are a divided people—
we are united—they quarrel about religion—we live in love and
friendship—they drink strong water—have learnt how to cheat—
and to practice all the vices of the white men, which disgrace
Indians, without imitating the virtues of the white men. Brother,
if you are our well wisher, keep away and do not disturb us.

"Brother—We do not worship the Great Spirit as the white
men do, but we believe that forms of worship are indifferent to
the Great Spirit—it is the offering of a sincere heart that pleases
him, and we worship him in this manner. According to your
religion we must believe in a father and a son, or we will not be
happy hereafter. We have always believed in a father, and we
worship him, as we were taught by our fathers. Your book says the
Son was sent on earth by the father—did all the people who saw
the son believe in him? No, they did not, and the consequences
must be known to you, if you have read the book.

"Brother: You wish us to change our religion for yours—we
like our religion and do not wish another. Our friends (Pointing
to Mr. Granger, the Agent of the United States for Indian affairs,
who was present; Mr. Parish, the Indian interpreter; and Mr. Taylor, the agent of the Society of Friends for Improving the Condition of the Indians, residing near the Alleghany settlement, but
also present at the Council) do us great good—they council us in
our troubles—and instruct us how to make ourselves comfortable.
Our friends the Quakers do more than this—they give us ploughs,
and show us how to use them. They tell us we are accountable
beings, but do not say we must change our religion. We are
satisfied with what they do.

"Brother: For these reasons we cannot receive your offers—we
have other things to do, and beg you to make your mind easy, and
not trouble us, lest our heads should be too much loaded, and by
and by burst."

APPENDIX E

——

Speech to Mr. Richardson, 1811

SPEECH OF RED JACKET

In answer to a speech of Mr. Richardson, who applied to buy the Indian rights to the reservations lying in the territory commonly called the Holland Purchase. Delivered at a council held at Buffalo Creek in May, 1811.

"Brother—We opened our ears to the talk you lately delivered to us, at our council fire. In doing important business it is best not to tell long stories, but to come to it in a few words. We therefore shall not repeat your talk, which is fresh in our minds. We have well considered it, and the advantages and disadvantages of your offers. We request your attention to our answer, which is not from the speaker alone, but from all the Sachems and Chiefs now around our council fire.

"Brother—We know that great men as well as great nations, having different interests have different minds, and do not see the same subject in the same light—but we hope our answer will be agreeable to you and to your employers.

"Brother—Your application for the purchase of our lands is to our minds very extraordinary. It has been made in a crooked manner—you have not walked in the straight path pointed out by the great Council of your nation. You have no writings from the President.

Reprinted from the *American Speaker* (1816), pages 379–81.

"Brother—In making up our minds we have looked back, and remembered how the Yorkers purchased our lands in former times. They bought them piece by piece for a little money paid to a few men in our nation, and not to all our brethren; our planting and hunting grounds have become very small, and if we sell these we know not where to spread our blankets.

"Brother—You tell us your employers have purchased of the Council of Yorkers a right to buy our lands—we do not understand how this can be—the lands do not belong to the Yorkers; they are ours, and were given to us by the Great Spirit.

"Brother—We think it strange that you should jump over the lands of our brethren in the East, to come to our Council fire so far off, to get our lands. When we sold our lands in the East to the white people, we determined never to sell those we kept, which are as small as we can live comfortably on.

"Brother—You want us to travel with you, and look for other lands. If we should sell our lands and move off into a distant country, toward the setting sun, we should be looked upon in the country to which we go as foreigners, and strangers, and be despised by the red as well as the white men, and we should soon be surrounded by the white men, who will there also kill our game, come upon our lands, and try to get them from us.

"Brother—We are determined not to sell our lands, but to continue on them—we like them—they are fruitful and produce us corn in abundance, for the support of our women and children, and grass and herbs for our cattle.

"Brother—At the treaties held for the purchase of our lands, the white man with sweet voices and smiling faces told us they loved us, and that they would not cheat us, but that the king's children on the other side of the lake would cheat us. When we go on the other side of the lake the king's children tell us your people will cheat us, but with sweet voices and smiling faces assure us of their love and they will not cheat us. These things puzzle our heads, and we believe that the Indians must take care of themselves, and not trust either in your people or in the king's children.

"Brother—At a late Council we requested our agents to tell you that we would not sell our lands, and we think you have not spoke to our agents, or they would have informed you so, and we should not have met you at our Council fire at this time.

"Brother—The white people buy and sell false rights to our lands; your employers have, you say, paid a great price for their right; they must have plenty of money, to spend it in buying false right to lands belonging to the Indians; the loss of it will not hurt them, but our lands are of great value to us, and we wish you to go back with your talk to your employers, and to tell them and the Yorkers that they have no right to buy and sell false rights to our lands.

"Brother—We hope you clearly understand the words we have spoken. This is all we have to say."

Bibliography

Newspapers

Albany Argus, 1829
Albany Centinel, 1801–2
Black Rock (N.Y.) *Gazette,* 1825–27
Buffalo Commercial Advertiser, 1852
Buffalo Daily Courier, 1851–52
Buffalo Express, 1897
Cherry Valley (N.Y.) *Gazette,* 1818
Geneva (N.Y.) *Gazette,* 1891
Geneva (N.Y.) *Palladium,* 1821–28
National Intelligencer (Washington, D.C.), 1811
New York Evening Post, 1829
New York Spectator, 1829
Ontario Repository (Canandaigua, N.Y.), 1809
Otsego Republican Press (Cherry Valley, N.Y.), 1812–13
Palmyra (N.Y.) *Register,* 1818
Rochester Daily Advertiser and Telegraph, 1830
Rochester Gem, 1830
Rochester Observer, 1830

Periodicals

American Missionary Register (New York, N.Y.) 1–4 (1821–23)
American Register (Philadelphia, Pa.) (1807–11)
Army and Navy Chronicle (Washington, D.C.) 5 (1837)

Boston Recorder (Boston, Mass.) 2–4, 19 (1817–19, 1833)
Christian Philanthropist (New Bedford, Mass.) 1 (1822)
Gospel Advocate (Buffalo, N.Y.) 1–5 (1823–27)
Massachusetts Missionary Magazine (Boston, Mass.) 1–5 (1803–8)
Missionary Herald (Boston, Mass.) (1821–31)
Monthly Anthology and Boston Review (Boston, Mass.), 6 (1809)
New England Galaxy (Boston, Mass.) 16 (1833)
New York Missionary Magazine (New York) 2–4 (1801–3)
New York State Assembly Journal (1824)
Niles Weekly Register (Baltimore, Md.) (1820–30)
Panoplist (Boston, Mass.) 2 (1806–7)
The Philanthropist (Mountpleasant, Ohio) 6 (1821)
Plain Truth (Canandaigua, N.Y.) 1 (1822)
Port Folio (Philadelphia, Pa.) 5 (1811)
Reformer (Philadelphia, Pa) (1820–31)
Western Recorder (Utica, N.Y.) (1824)

Books and Articles

Abler, Thomas S., ed. 1989. *Chainbreaker: The Revolutionary War Memoirs of Governor Blacksnake.* Lincoln: Univ. of Nebraska Press.
Adkins, Nelson Frederick. 1930. *Fitz-Green Halleck: An Early Knickerbocker Wit and Poet.* New Haven, Conn.:Yale Univ. Press.
Alden, Timothy. 1827. *An Account of Sundry Missions among the Senecas and Munsees.* New York: J. Seymour.
Allen, Robert S. 1975. *The British Indian Department and the Frontier in North America, 1775–1830.* Ottawa, Ontario: National Historic Parks and Sites Branch, Parks Canada, Indian and Northern Affairs.
———. 1992. *His Majesty's Indian Allies: British Indian Policy in the Defense of Canada, 1774–1815.* Toronto: Dundurn Press.
American Speaker. 1816. 3d ed. Philadelphia: Abraham Small.
American State Papers. Documents, Legislative and Executive, of the Congress of the United States: Indian Affairs. 1832. Edited by Walter Lowrie and Matthew St. Clair Clarke. 2 vols. Washington, D.C.: Gales and Seaton.
Armstrong, William H. 1974. "Red Jacket's Medal: An American Badge of Nobility." *Niagara Frontier* 21:26–36.

Babcock, Louis L. 1927. *The War of 1812 on the Niagara Frontier.* Buffalo, N.Y.: Buffalo Historical Society.

Barton, James L. 1879. "Early Reminiscences of Buffalo and Vicinity." *Publications of the Buffalo Historical Society* 1:153–78.

Barton, Lois. 1990. *A Quaker Promise Kept: Philadelphia Friends Work with the Alleghany Senecas, 1795–1960.* Eugene, Oreg.: Spencer Butte Press.

Benn, Carl. 1991. "Iroquois Warfare, 1812–1814." In *War along the Niagara: Essays on the War of 1812 and Its Legacy,* edited by R. Arthur Bowler, 60–76. Youngstown, N.Y.: Old Fort Niagara Association.

———. 1996. "The Iroquois Nadir of 1796." In *Niagara 1796: A Fortress Possessed,* 50–58. Youngstown, N.Y.: Old Fort Niagara Association.

Bingham, Robert W. 1931. *The Cradle of the Queen City: A History of Buffalo to the Incorporation of the City.* Buffalo, N.Y.: Buffalo Historical Society.

———. "Reports of Joseph Ellicott." *Publications of the Buffalo Historical Society* 32.

Blanchard, Rufus. 1880. *The Discovery and Conquest of the Northwest.* Chicago: Cushing, Thomas.

Bryant, William C. 1879. "Orlando Allen: Glimpses of Life in the Village of Buffalo." *Publications of the Buffalo Historical Society* 1:329–71.

Buchanan, James, 1824. *Sketches of the History, Manners, and Customs of the North American Indians.* New York: W. Borradaile.

Buffalo Historical Society. 1885. "Red Jacket." *Transactions of the Buffalo Historical Society* 3.

———. 1893. *Annual Report of the Board of Managers of the Buffalo Historical Society.* Buffalo, N.Y.: Buffalo Historical Society.

Calhoun, John C. 1969–74. *Papers of John C. Calhoun,* edited by W. Edwin Hemphill. Vols. 4–9. Columbia: Univ. of South Carolina Press.

Calloway, Colin G. 1987. *Crown and Calumet: British-Indian Relations, 1783–1815.* Norman: Univ. of Oklahoma Press.

Campbell, William W. 1849. *The Life and Writings of Dewitt Clinton.* New York: Baker and Scribner.

Campisi, Jack. 1988, "From Stanwix to Canandaigua: National Policy, States' Rights and Indian Land." In *Iroquois Land Claims*, edited by Christopher Vecsey and William A. Starna. Syracuse, N.Y.: Syracuse Univ. Press.

Campisi, Jack, and William A. Starna. 1995. "On the Road to Canandaigua: The Treaty of 1794." *American Indian Quarterly* 19:467–90.

Caswell, Harriet S. 1892. *Our Life Among the Iroquois Indians.* Boston, Mass.: Congregational Sunday School and Publishing Society.

Catlin, George. 1841. *Letters and Notes on the Manners, Customs, and Conditions of the North American Indians.* 2 vols. New York: Wiley and Putnam.

Chafe, Wallace L. 1967. *Seneca Morphology and Dictionary.* Washington, D.C.: Smithsonian Univ. Press.

Cleveland, Stafford C. 1873. *History and Directory of Yates County.* Penn Yan, N.Y.: S.C. Cleveland.

Conover, George S. 1884. *The Birth-Place of Sa-go-ye-wat-ha, or the Indian Red Jacket.* Waterloo, N.Y.: Seneca County News.

Costa Nunes, Jadviga da. 1980. "Red Jacket: The Man and His Portraits." *American Art Journal* 12:4–20.

Covell, Lemuel. 1804. *A Narrative of a Missionary Tour Through the Western Settlements of New-York, and into the South-western Parts of the Province of Upper Canada.* Troy, N.Y.: Moffitt and Lyon.

Cram, Jacob. 1909. *Journal of a Missionary Tour in 1808.* Rochester, N.Y.: Genesee Press.

Cumming, John. 1979. "A Missionary among the Seneca: The Journal of Abel Bingham, 1822–1828." *New York History* 60:157–93.

Dearborn, Henry A. S. 1904. "Journals of Henry A. S. Dearborn." *Publications of the Buffalo Historical Society* 7:33–225.

Delafield, John. 1850. "A General View and Agricultural Survey of the County of Seneca." *Transactions of the New York State Agricultural Society* 10:356–616.

Densmore, Christopher. 1987. "More on Red Jacket's Reply." *New York Folklore* 13:121–22.

Drake, Samuel G. 1880. *Aboriginal Races of North America.* 15th ed. New York: Hurst. First published in 1832 as *Indian Biography* and later revised as *Biography and History of the Indians of North America.*

Dunlap, William. 1834. *A History of the Rise and Progress of the Arts of Design in the United States.* 2 vols. New York: G. P. Scott.

Eckert, Allan W. 1992. *A Sorrow in Our Heart: The Life of Tecumseh.* New York: Bantam Books.

Edmunds, R. David. 1984. *Tecumseh and the Quest for Indian Leadership.* Boston: Little, Brown.

Emerson, Charles F. 1911. *General Catalogue of Dartmouth College.* Hanover, N.H.: Dartmouth.

Farmer's Brother. 1809. *Indian Speeches Delivered by Farmer's Brother and Red Jacket, Two Seneca Chiefs.* Canandaigua, N.Y.: James D. Bemis.

————. 1810. *Speeches Delivered by Several Indian Chiefs.* New York: Samuel Wood.

Fillmore, Millard. 1879. "Inaugural Address of Millard Fillmore [July 1, 1862, at the Buffalo Historical Society]," *Publications of the Buffalo Historical Society* 1:1–15.

Francello, Joseph A. 1989. *The Seneca Worlds of Go-no-Say-Yeh.* New York: Peter Lang.

Graymont, Barbara. 1972. *The Iroquois in the American Revolution.* Syracuse, N.Y.: Syracuse Univ. Press.

Guennsey, A. H. 1866. "The Red Jacket Medal." *Harpers New Monthly Magazine* 32:323–36.

Harris, George H. 1903. "The Life of Horatio Jones." *Publications of the Buffalo Historical Society* 6:381–514.

Harris, Thompson S. 1903. "Journals of Rev. Thompson S. Harris, Missionary to the Senecas." *Publications of the Buffalo Historical Society* 6:281–380.

Hauptman, Laurence M. 1988. "The Historical Background of the Present-Day Seneca Nation—Salamanca Lease Controversy," In *Iroquois Land Claims,* edited by Christopher Vecsey and William A. Starna, 101–22. Syracuse, N.Y.: Syracuse Univ. Press.

Horsman, Reginald. 1958. "British Indian Policy in the Northwest." *Mississippi Valley Historical Review* 45:51–66.

Howland, Henry R. 1903. "The Seneca Mission at Buffalo Creek." *Publications of the Buffalo Historical Society* 6:125–61.

Hubbard, John Niles. 1886. *An Account of Sa-go-ye-wat-ha, or Red Jacket and his People.* Albany, N.Y.: Munsell.

Hyde, Jabez B. 1903. "A Teacher among the Senecas: Narrative of Rev. Jabez Bacus Hyde." *Publications of the Buffalo Historical Society* 6:239–74.

Jahoda, Gloria. 1971. *The Trail of Tears.* New York: Holt, Rinehart and Winston.

Jennings, Francis, ed. 1985. *The History and Culture of Iroquois Diplomacy.* Syracuse, N.Y.: Syracuse Univ. Press.

Johnson, Crisfield. 1876. *Centennial History of Erie County, New York.* Buffalo, N.Y.: Matthews and Warren.

Johnston, Charles M., ed. 1964. *The Valley of the Six Nations: A Collection of Documents on the Indian Lands of the Grand River.* Toronto, Ontario: Champlain Society.

Kappler, Charles J., ed. 1904. *Indian Affairs: Laws and Treaties.* Compiled and edited by Charles J. Kappler. 2 vols. Washington, D.C.: Government Printing Office.

Kelsay, Isabel T. 1984. *Joseph Brant, 1743–1807: Man of Two Worlds.* Syracuse, N.Y.: Syracuse Univ. Press.

Ketcham, William. 1865. *An Authentic and Comprehensive History of Buffalo.* 2 vols. Buffalo, N.Y.: Rockwell, Baker and Hill.

Lankes, Frank J. 1957. "The Last Days of Red Jacket." *Niagara Frontier* 4:43–45.

Letchworth, William P. 1874. *Sketch of the Life of Samuel F. Pratt.* Buffalo, N.Y.: Warren, Johnson.

Levasseur, A. 1829. *Lafayette in America, in 1824 and 1825, or, Journal of Travels in the United States.* 2 vols. New York: White, Gallaher and White.

Lincoln, Charles A., ed. 1909. *Messages from the Governor.* Vol. 2. Albany, N.Y.: J. B. Lyon.

Lundy's Lane Historical Society. 1971. *The Documentary History of the Campaign on the Niagara Frontier.* New York: Arno. 1896–1908. Reprint, edited by E. A. Cruikshank.

McKenney, Thomas L. 1967. *Biographical Sketches and Anecdotes of Ninety-five of the Principal Chiefs from the Indian Tribes of North America.* Washington: U.S. Department of the Interior, Bureau of Indian Affairs. 1838. Reprint, vol. 1, *History of the Indian Tribes of North America.* Philadelphia.

McKenney, Thomas L. and James Hall. 1838–44. *History of the Indian Tribes of North America.* 3 vols. Philadelphia: F. W. Greenough.

Manley, Henry S. 1950. "Red Jacket's Last Campaign." *New York History* 31:149–68.

Minard, John S. 1888. *Hume Pioneer Sketches.* Fillmore, N.Y.: Northern Allegany Observer.

Moore, Joseph. 1835. *Joseph Moore's Journal of a Tour to Detroit, in Order to Attend a Treaty, Proposed to be Held with the Indians at Sandusky.* In *Friends Miscellany* 6:289–343.

Morgan, Lewis Henry. 1851. *League of the Ho-Dé-No-Sau-Nee, Iroquois.* Rochester: Sage and Brother.

———. 1965. *Houses and House-life of the American Aborigines.* Chicago: Univ. of Chicago Press. Originally published IN 1881 in vol. 4, *Contributions to North American Ethnology.*

Nevins, Allan, ed. 1928. *The Diary of John Quincy Adams, 1794–1845.* New York: Longmans, Green.

New York State. 1822. *Laws of the State of New-York, Passed at the Forty-Fifth Session of the Legislature.* Albany: Cantine and Leake.

———. 1829. *Revised Statutes of the State of New-York.* 3 vols. Albany: Parkard and Van Benthuysen.

———. 1909. *Messages from the Governors*, edited by Charles Z. Lincoln. Albany: Published by authority of the State.

Norton, John. 1970. *The Journal of Major John Norton, 1816.* Toronto: Champlain Society.

Odell, George C. D. 1928. *Annals of the New York Stage.* Vol. 3. New York: Columbia Univ. Press.

O'Reilly, Henry O. 1838. *Sketches of Rochester.* Rochester, N.Y.: William Alling.

Parker, Arthur C. 1913. *The Code of Handsome Lake, the Seneca Prophet.* New York State Museum Bulletin, 163. Albany: University of the State of New York.

———. 1916a. *The Constitution of the Five Nations or the Iroquois Book of the Great Law.* New York State Museum Bulletin, 184. Albany: Univ. of the State of New York.

———. 1916b. "The Senecas in the War of 1812." *Proceedings of the New York State Historical Association* 15:78–90.

———. 1919. *The Life of General Ely S. Parker.* Buffalo, N.Y.: Buffalo Historical Society.

———. 1943. "The Unknown Mother of Red Jacket." *New York History* 24:525–33.

————. 1952. *Red Jacket: Last of the Seneca.* New York: McGraw-Hill.

Parker, Ely S. 1885. "Red Jacket's Disappointed Ambition." *Transactions of the Buffalo Historical Society* 3:66–70.

Pedersen, Gilbert J. 1956. "Early Title to the Indian Reservations in Western New York." *Niagara Frontier* 3:5–12.

Pennsylvania. 1853. *Minutes of the Supreme Executive Council of Pennsylvania.* Vol. 16, 1789–90. Harrisburg: T. Fenn.

Pickering, Octavius. 1867–73. *Life of Timothy Pickering.* 4 vols. Boston, Mass.: Little, Brown.

Prucha, Francis P. 1971. *Indian Peace Medals in American History.* Lincoln: Univ. of Nebraska Press.

Red Jacket. 1811. *Native Eloquence: Being Public Speeches Delivered by Two Distinguished Chiefs of the Seneca Tribe of Indians, Known among the White People by the Names of Red Jacket and Farmer's Brother.* Canandaigua, N.Y.: J. D. Bemis.

————. 1912. *A Long-Lost Speech of Red Jacket.* Friendship, N.Y.: J. W. Sanborn.

———— [pseud.]. 1830? *First Impressions on Reading the Message of the Governor of Georgia, 1830, Relative to the Indians.* N.p.

Register of Debates in Congress [1824–37]. Washington, D.C.: Gales and Seaton.

Robie, Harry. 1986. "Red Jacket's Reply: Problems in the Verification of a Native American Speech Text." *New York Folklore* 12:99–117.

Savery, William. 1837. "A Journal of the Life, Travels and Religious Labours of William Savery." In *Friends Library* 1:325–459.

Schoolcraft, Henry R. 1847. *Notes on the Iroquois.* Rochester, N.Y.: Erastus H. Pease.

Seaver, James E. 1990. *A Narrative of the Life of Mrs. Mary Jemison.* Syracuse, N.Y.: Syracuse Univ. Press.

Severance, Frank H. 1896. "The First Buffalo Book." *Publications of the Buffalo Historical Society* 4:385–414. Includes facsimile reprint of *Public Speeches, Delivered at the Village of Buffalo, on the 6th and 8th Days of July, 1812, by Erastus Granger, Indian Agent, and Red Jacket, One of the Principal Chiefs and Speakers of the Seneca Nation, Respecting the Part the Six Nations Would Take in the Present War Against Great Britain.* Buffalo: S. H. and H. A. Salisbury, 1812.

————. 1921. "The Red Jacket Relics." *Publications of the Buffalo Historical Society* 25:233–42

Shackford, James A. 1956. *David Crockett: The Man and the Legend.* Edited by John B. Shackford. Chapel Hill: Univ. of North Carolina Press.

Simcoe, John Graves. 1923–31. *The Correspondence of Lieut. Governor John Graves Simcoe.* Edited by E. A. Cruikshank. 5 vols. Toronto: Ontario Historical Society.

Simms, Jeptha R. 1882–83. *The Frontiersmen of New York.* Albany, N.Y.: G. C. Riggs.

Snow, Dean R. 1994. *The Iroquois.* Cambridge, Mass.: Blackwell Publishers.

Snyder, Charles M. 1978. *Red and White on the New York Frontier: A Struggle for Survival.* Harrison, N.Y.: Harbor Hill Books.

Sparks, Jared, ed. 1853. *Correspondence of the American Revolution.* Vol. 4. Boston: Little, Brown.

Stanley, George F. G. 1950. "The Indians in the War of 1812." *Canadian Historical Review* 31:145–65.

————. 1963. "The Significance of the Six Nations Participation in the War of 1812." *Ontario History* 55:215–31.

Starna, William A. 1988. "Aboriginal Title and Traditional Iroquois Land Use: An Anthropological Perspective." In *Iroquois Land Claims,* edited by Christopher Vecsey and William A. Starna, 31–48. Syracuse, N.Y.: Syracuse Univ. Press.

Stone, William L. 1838. *Life of Joseph Brant—Thayendanega.* 2 vols. New York: Alexander V. Blake.

————. 1841. *Life and Times of Red-Jacket.* New York: Wiley and Putnam.

————. 1866. *The Life and Times of Sa-go-ye-wat-ha, or Red Jacket.* Albany, N.Y.: J. Munsell.

Stork, William V. 1898. *The Student's Handbook of Yates County.* Penn Yan, N.Y.: Express Book and Job Print.

Strong, Nathaniel T. 1879. "Correspondence on the Name of Buffalo." *Publications of the Buffalo Historical Society* 1:38–42.

Tanner, Helen H., ed. 1987. *Atlas of Great Lakes Indian History.* Norman: Univ. of Oklahoma Press.

Thatcher, B. B. 1840. *Indian Biography.* 2 vols. New York: Harper and Brothers.

Thwaites, Reuben G., and Louise P. Kellogg. 1908. *The Revolution on the Upper Ohio, 1775–1777.* Madison: Wisconsin Historical Society.

Tucker, Glenn. 1956. *Tecumseh: Vision of Glory.* Indianapolis, Ind.: Bobbs-Merrill.

Turner, O. 1850. *Pioneer History of the Holland Purchase of Western New York.* Buffalo, N.Y.: George Derby.

————. 1851. *History of the Pioneer Settlement of Phelps and Gorham's Purchase.* Rochester, N.Y.: William Alling.

Upton, Helen C. 1980. *The Everett Report in Historical Perspective: The Indians of New York.* New York: New York State American Revolution Bicentennial Commission.

Vecsey, Christopher, and William Starna, eds. 1988. *Iroquois Land Claims.* Syracuse, N.Y.: Syracuse Univ. Press.

Venables, Robert W., ed. 1995. *The Six Nations of New York: The 1892 United States Extra Census Bulletin.* Ithaca, N.Y.: Cornell Univ. Press.

Wallace, Anthony F. C. 1972. *The Death and Rebirth of the Seneca.* New York: Vintage Books.

Waterloo Library and Historical Society. 1892. *Unveiling of the Monument Erected by the Waterloo Library and Historical Society, as a Memorial to Red Jacket, Sa-go-ya-wat-ha, at Canoga, New York, the Place of His Birth, Oct. 14, 1891.* Waterloo, N.Y.: Waterloo Library and Historical Society.

Wilkinson, Norman B. 1953. "Robert Morris and the Treaty of Big Tree." *Mississippi Valley Historical Review* 40:257–78.

Wilson, James G. 1869. *The Life and Letters of Fitz-Greene Halleck.* New York: D. Appleton.

Wisby, Herbert A. 1958. "J. L. D. Mathies, Western New York Artist." *New York History* 39:133–50.

Manuscripts

Aigin, James. Reminiscences of Buffalo. Buffalo and Erie County Historical Society, Buffalo, N.Y.

Draper Manuscripts. State Historical Society of Wisconsin, Madison, Wisconsin.

Holland Land Company. Archives of the Holland Land Company, 1798–1869. Microfilmed by the State University of New York at Fredonia from the originals in the Municipal Archives of Amsterdam, The Netherlands.

Indian Collection. 1788–1955. Buffalo and Erie County Historical Society, Buffalo, N.Y.

Marshall Family. Marshall Family Papers. 1762–1908. State University of New York at Oswego. Includes papers of Erastus Granger. Oswego, N.Y.

New York State Legislature. Petitions, Correspondence and Reports Relating to Indians. 1783–1831. New York State Archives, A 1823. Albany, N.Y.

Ogden Land Company. Record Book 1811–82. New York State Library, Albany, N.Y. No. 8348. Albany, N.Y.

O'Reilly, Henry. Henry O'Reilly Collection: Papers Relating to the Six Nations. New-York Historical Society, New York City. Includes "Pioneer Settlements" (1844) and other papers of Thomas Morris.

Parker Family Papers. 1836–1903. Buffalo and Erie County Historical Society (BHS), ms. A64 94. Buffalo, N.Y.

Pickering, Timothy. Papers. Massachusetts Historical Society, Boston, Massachusetts.

Pierce, Maris B. Papers. Buffalo and Erie County Historical Society, Buffalo, N.Y.

Porter, Peter B. Peter B. Porter Papers. Buffalo and Erie County Historical Society, Buffalo, N.Y.

Society of Friends. New York Yearly Meeting. Indian Committee. Friends Historical Library, Swarthmore College. Swarthmore, Pennsylvania.

———. Philadelphia Yearly Meeting. Indian Committee. Records, 1757–1895. Quakea Collection, Haverford College, Haverford, Pennsylvania.

Strong, Nathaniel T. 1863. Speech on Red Jacket. Buffalo and Erie County Historical Society, Buffalo, N.Y.

United States. Records of the Office of the Secretary of War Relating to Indian Affairs. Letters Received, 1800–23. National Archives Microfilm, M 271, roll 1–4.

———. Records of the Office of the Secretary of War Relating to Indian Affairs. Letters Sent, 1800–24. National Archives Microfilm, M 15, roll 1–6.

———. War Department. Office of Indian Affairs. Letters Received. Seneca Agency in New York, 1824–32. National Archives Microfilm, M 234, roll 808.

———. War Department. Office of Indian Affairs. Letters Received. Six Nations Agency, 1824–1834. National Archives Microfilm, M 234, roll 832.

———. War Department. Office of Indian Affairs. Letters Sent, 1824–30. National Archives Microfilm, M 21, roll 1–6.

Index